THE
QUOTABLE NICHIREN

THE
QUOTABLE
NICHIREN

Words

for

Daily

Living

World Tribune
Press

Published by World Tribune Press
606 Wilshire Boulevard
Santa Monica, CA 90401

The excerpts of the writings of Nichiren quoted or paraphrased
in this book are from *The Writings of Nichiren Daishonin*, © 1999
by Soka Gakkai, published in 1999 by Soka Gakkai, and used with
permission of the Soka Gakkai. Occasionally, some quotations
have been slightly modified in order to increase their clarity.

Printed in the U.S.A.

Interior illustrations by Ed Lee
Interior and cover designed by Lightbourne, LLC

10 9 8 7 6 5 4 3 2

Library of Congress Cataloging-in-Publication Data

Nichiren, 1222-1282.
    Quotable Nichiren : words for daily living / by World
Tribune Press.
        p. cm.
    ISBN 0-915678-97-7 (Hardcover : alk. paper)
    1. Nichiren, 1222-1282--Quotations. 2. Nichiren (Sect)--
Doctrines. I. Title.
    BQ8349.N572 2003
    294.3'928--dc21

                                            2003008858

CONTENTS

LIST OF ILLUSTRATIONS

(in order of appearance)

FOREWORD

Matilda Buck, SGI-USA Women's Leader
Danny Nagashima, SGI-USA General Director

NICHIREN'S WRITINGS are so practical and humanistic that for centuries people have engraved even just a sentence or two as guiding principles for their lives. As Nichiren said: "Teach others to the best of your ability, even if it is only a single sentence or phrase." In today's hectic world, a single phrase is often the only thing we have time to read. Hence this book.

We are very excited about the publishing of *The Quotable Nichiren* because Nichiren's most touching words are now more accessible through this portable reference. Though written more than 700 years ago, his words are as relevant today as they were then. Whether we seek inspiration, philosophy, common sense, quiet reflection or tenderness, we can find it in his words. Through his conviction we can find inspiration to surmount everyday problems. Moreover, he offers clear advice on how to live a life of self-reliance and contribution.

Years ago, Danny created his own collection of Nichiren's quotes and refers to it continually, so he knows first-hand how invaluable a reference like *The Quotable Nichiren* can be. In any case, both of us hope this book will become a precious tool for you to use over and over again.

The editors have selected more than 700 quotes and arranged them by subject, making it easy for you to find just what you need to encourage yourself or a friend. They made special effort to select quotes particularly relevant to daily living. This includes famous passages that are not always easy to find. Important quotes from Nichiren's longer treatises and theoretical works are also included.

Interesting facts, essential points of practice, and key figures in the life and times of Nichiren are featured in boxes throughout the book, helping us see how Nichiren's writings can relate to our lives. More than a dozen beautiful illustrations by Ed Lee give us a look into the 13th-century times of Nichiren.

So browse *The Quotable Nichiren*, carry it with you and refer to it often, for as SGI President Ikeda reminds us, "even if you forget what you've read, something profound will have been engraved in the depths of your life."

Enjoy this book.

EDITOR'S NOTE

We've compiled this book for all those who might find the entirety of Nichiren's works (Gosho) a bit dense to plunge into, as well as for those whose *The Writings of Nichiren Daishonin* is filled with dog-eared pages, underlined passages and scribbled notes written in the margins.

For those new to Nichiren Buddhism, you'll find hundreds of important passages that give you a great overview of Nichiren's philosophy and how it can benefit your daily life. For the more seasoned practitioner, *The Quotable Nichiren* contains many of the passages you've heard or read countless times over the years, all arranged by topic. Moreover, each selection contains a page reference to *The Writings of Nichiren Daishonin* (abbreviated WND), so in case you're inspired to explore more, you can easily find it in context. (A handful of quotes come from The *Gosho Zenshu*, abbreviated GZ, the Japanese-language compilation of Nichiren's works.)

As for any such work that selects passages from a larger body of writings, this book relies on the subjectivity of those who compiled this book. You may not find your favorite passage, but you may see something you've never read before. In any case, we trust these bite-sized quotes, each an independent and compelling thought, can be the fuel for your practice.

To enhance this collection, we have added dozens of small boxes throughout the text in four categories. "Reflections" presents short quotes from SGI President Daisaku Ikeda and Second Soka Gakkai President Josei Toda. These quotes share these great teachers' thoughts on the importance of the writings. In "Fast Facts" we highlight some interesting tidbits relating to the life and times of Nichiren. "People to Know" features important people in Nichiren's life, and "Faith in Daily Life" introduces essential Buddhist concepts that explore how these 700-year-old writings matter to your twenty-first-century life.

Because any one quote could be categorized in more than one topic, we've also provided a complete subject index to make it even easier to find just the passage you're looking for. There are also useful appendices in the back. Finally, we would like to thank our illustrator, Ed Lee, for sharing his conception of what life looked like in Japan during Nichiren's time.

We hope you will enjoy this book for years to come.

The Editors
World Tribune Press

ACTION

Because you have read the entirety of the Lotus Sutra with both the physical and spiritual aspects of your life, you will also be able to save your father and mother, your six kinds of relatives, and all living beings. Others read the Lotus Sutra with their mouths alone, in word alone, but they do not read it with their hearts. And even if they read it with their hearts, they do not read it with their actions. It is reading the sutra with both one's body and mind that is truly praiseworthy! (WND, 204)

Those at the stage of being a Buddha in theory only and at the stage of hearing the name and words of the truth believe in the perfect teaching; but even though they praise it, their actions fail to reflect their words. (WND, 199–200)

Though some people wish to help me, either their determination is weak, or, though firmly resolved, they are unable to act on their intentions. Thus, you are one of the very few whose actions match their will. (WND, 753)

"How great is the difference between the blessings received when a sage chants the daimoku and the blessings received when we chant it?" To reply, one is in no way superior to the other. The gold that a fool possesses is no different from the gold that a wise man possesses; a fire made by a fool is the same as a fire made by a wise man. However, there is a difference if one chants the daimoku while acting against the intent of this sutra. (WND, 756)

ACTUAL PROOF

Therefore, I say to you, my disciples, try practicing as the Lotus Sutra teaches, exerting yourselves without begrudging your lives! Test the truth of Buddhism now! (WND, 583–84)

In judging the relative merit of Buddhist doctrines, I, Nichiren, believe that the best standards are those of reason and documentary proof. And even more valuable than reason and documentary proof is the proof of actual fact. (WND, 599)

In light of all this, it would seem that, when one who is able to show clearly visible proof in the present expounds the Lotus Sutra, there also will be persons who will believe. (WND, 512)

Nothing is more certain than actual proof. (WND, 478)

ANGER

Your face bears definite signs of a hot temper. But you should know that the heavenly gods will not protect a short-tempered person, however important they may think he or she is. (WND, 849)

Since you are hot-tempered and behave like a blazing fire, you will certainly be deceived by others. If your lord coaxes you with soft words, I am sure you will be won over, just as a fire is extinguished by water. Untempered iron quickly melts in a blazing fire, like ice put in hot water. But a sword, even when exposed to a great fire, withstands the heat for a while, because it has been well forged. In admonishing you in this way, I am trying to forge your faith. (WND, 839)

Famine occurs as a result of greed, pestilence as a result of foolishness, and warfare as a result of anger. (WND, 989)

When Hei no Saemon and Akitajo-no-suke, in their anger, wreak havoc upon us, you must demonstrate a firm resolve. (WND, 997)

Many people have plotted to undo you, but you have avoided their intrigues and emerged victorious. Should you lose your composure now and fall into their trap, you will be, as people say, like a boatman who rows his boat with all his might only to have it capsize just before he reaches the shore. (WND, 849)

Reflections

WISDOM

"It is imperative that you have wisdom. For that reason, it is vital that, based on chanting daimoku, you study diligently, starting with the Daishonin's teachings. It is essential that you develop and strengthen your intellect."

—Daisaku Ikeda

APPRECIATION

As for my parents in this lifetime, however, they not only gave me birth but made me a believer in the Lotus Sutra. Thus I owe my present father and mother a debt far greater than I would had I been born into the family of Brahma, Shakra, one of the four heavenly kings, or a wheel-turning king, and so inherited the threefold world or the four continents, and been revered by the four kinds of believers in the worlds of human and heavenly beings. (WND, 44)

The wise may be called human, but the thoughtless are no more than animals. (WND, 852)

The old fox never forgets the hillock where he was born; the white turtle repaid the kindness he had received from Mao Pao. If even lowly creatures know enough to do this, then how much more should human beings! (WND, 690)

When I attain Buddhahood, how will I be able to forget my obligation to Sho-bo? Much less can I forget the thanks I owe to the scroll of the Lotus Sutra [with which he struck me]. When I think of this, I cannot restrain my tears of gratitude. (WND, 964)

ARROGANCE

There was something very strange about Sammi-bo. Nevertheless, I was concerned that any admonition would be taken by the ignorant as mere jealousy of his wisdom, and so I refrained from speaking out. In time his wicked ambition led to treachery and, finally, to his doom. If I had scolded him more strictly, he might have been saved. I have not mentioned this before because no one would have understood it. Even now the ignorant will say that I am

People to Know

SIX SENIOR PRIESTS

Of Nichiren's six main disciples, only Nikko remained loyal to the very end. The other five priests—Nissho, Nichiro, Niko, Nitcho and Nichiji—strayed from Nichiren's teachings after his death and declared themselves followers of another sect.

speaking ill of the deceased. Nevertheless, I mention it so that others can use it as their mirror. (WND, 998)

Among the non-Buddhist believers of India there have been men who could pour all the waters of the Ganges River into their ear and keep it there for twelve years, or those who could drink the ocean dry, grasp the sun and moon in their hands, or change the disciples of Shakyamuni Buddha into oxen or sheep. But such powers only made them more arrogant than ever and caused them to create further karma to confine themselves in the sufferings of birth and death. (WND, 723)

Since we are now living in the latter age when people are shallow in wisdom and puffed up with pride, it is unlikely that anyone will heed the points I have made in the discussion above. But when a sage or worthy appears, then the full truth of the matter will no doubt become clear. (WND, 868)

No matter how humble a person may be, if his wisdom is the least bit greater than yours, you should ask him about the meaning of the sutra. But the people in this evil age are so arrogant, prejudiced, and attached to fame and profit that they are afraid that, should they become the disciple of a humble person or try to learn something from him, they will be looked down upon by others. They never rid themselves of this wrong attitude, so they seem to be destined for the evil paths. (WND, 757)

Now, if you wish to attain Buddhahood, you have only to lower the banner of your arrogance, cast aside the staff of your anger, and devote yourself exclusively to the one vehicle of the Lotus Sutra. Worldly fame and profit are mere baubles of your present existence, and arrogance and prejudice are ties that will fetter you in the next one. (WND, 58–59)

There are a few in this province of Kai who have expressed their desire to take faith. Yet I make it a rule not to permit them to join us unless they remain steadfast in their resolve. Some people, despite their

Reflections

UNIVERSAL PRINCIPLES

"The Daishonin's writings also reflect the cultural and social conditions of his time. Nevertheless, universal principles both timeless and unchanging are beautifully expressed therein. Our responsibility, I believe, is to read and extract those principles, and bring them to life in the present." —Daisaku Ikeda shallow understanding, pretend staunch faith and speak contemptuously to their fellow believers, thus often disrupting the faith of others. (WND, 800)

When you look at those of superior capacity, do not disparage yourself. The Buddha's true intention was that no one, even those of inferior capacity, be denied enlightenment. Conversely, when you compare yourself with persons of inferior capacity, do not be arrogant and overproud. Even persons of superior capacity may be excluded from enlightenment if they do not devote themselves wholeheartedly. (WND, 62)

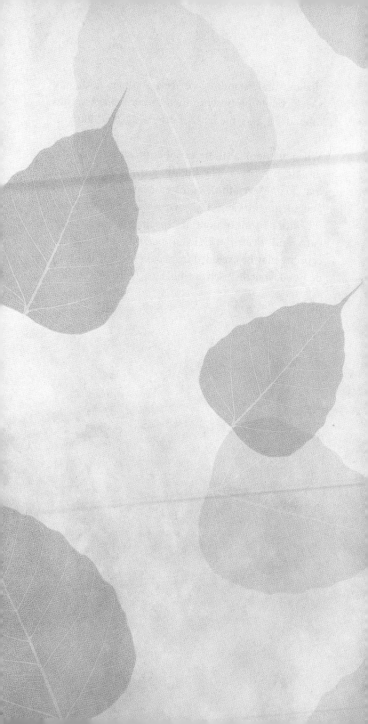

BEHAVIOR

The heart of the Buddha's lifetime of teachings is the Lotus Sutra, and the heart of the practice of the Lotus Sutra is found in the "Never Disparaging" chapter. What does Bodhisattva Never Disparaging's profound respect for people signify? The purpose of the appearance in this world of Shakyamuni Buddha, the lord of teachings, lies in his behavior as a human being. (WND, 851–52)

If they have eyes, they should examine the sutra texts and compare their own behavior with them. (WND, 276)

The Great Teacher Dengyo states that the otter shows its respect by offering up the fish it has caught, the crow in the forest carries food to its parents and grandparents, the dove takes care to perch three branches lower than its father, wild geese keep perfect formation when they fly together, and lambs kneel to drink their mother's milk. He asks: if lowly animals conduct themselves with such propriety, how can human beings be so lacking in courtesy? (WND, 1031)

Take these teachings to heart, and always remember that believers in the Lotus Sutra should absolutely be the last to abuse one another. (WND, 756)

People to Know

IKEGAMI BROTHERS

Munenaka and Munenaga were two brothers that held firm in their allegiance to Nichiren. They both took up faith despite their father's strong opposition. Nichiren advised them to unite as a family and maintain their faith. In the end, though the father had been a loyal follower of Ryokan, he converted to Nichiren's teachings.

Thus even a ruler on a throne must take care not to give unreserved expression to his thoughts. The worthy man Confucius held to his belief "Nine thoughts to one word," which means that he reconsidered nine times before he spoke. Tan, the Duke of Chou, was so earnest in receiving callers that he would wring out his hair three times in the course of washing it, or spit out his food three times in the course of a meal [in order not to keep them waiting]. Consider this carefully so that you will have no cause to reproach me later. What is called Buddhism is found in this behavior. (WND, 851)

Bodhisattva Never Disparaging of old said that all people have the Buddha nature and that, if they embrace the Lotus Sutra, they will never fail to attain Buddhahood. He further stated that to slight a person is to slight the Buddha himself. Thus, his practice was to revere all people. He revered even those who did not embrace the Lotus Sutra because they too had the Buddha nature and might someday believe in the sutra. (WND, 756)

BENEFIT

By considering the magnitude of the punishment suffered by those who harbor enmity toward the Lotus Sutra, we can understand the magnitude of the benefits obtained by devoting oneself to it. (WND, 1095)

Those who obtained benefit during the Former and Middle Days of the Law received "conspicuous" benefit, because the relationship they formed with the Lotus Sutra during the lifetime of the Buddha had finally matured. On the other hand, those born today in the Latter Day of the Law receive the seeds of Buddhahood for the first time, and their benefit is therefore "inconspicuous." (WND, 474)

Just as I was thinking that, even if I remained free from illness, I would surely die of starvation, the wheat that you sent arrived. It is more wonderful than gold and more precious than jewels. Rida's millet changed into a golden man. How, then, could Tokimitsu's wheat fail to turn into the characters of the Lotus Sutra? These characters of the Lotus Sutra will become Shakyamuni Buddha and then a pair of wings for your deceased father, flying and soaring to the pure land of Eagle Peak. On returning, they will cover your body and protect you. (WND, 926)

Shakyamuni's practices and the virtues he consequently attained are all contained within the five characters of Myoho-renge-kyo. If we believe in these five characters, we will naturally be granted the same benefits as he was. (WND, 365)

The Buddha wisdom is so marvelous that it knows even the number of raindrops that fall in this major world system during a period, for instance, of seven days or twice seven days. And yet we read that the blessings acquired by one who recites no more than a single word of the Lotus Sutra are the one thing it cannot fathom. How, then, could ordinary people like ourselves, who have committed grave offenses, possibly understand these blessings? (WND, 68)

If a spark as small as a bean is set to a single blade of grass in a spring field of a thousand square *ri* thick with grass, it becomes in an instant an immeasurable, boundless blaze. Such is also the case with this robe [you have offered]. Though only one robe, it has been offered to the Buddhas of all the characters of the Lotus Sutra. Be firmly convinced that the benefits from this will extend to your parents, your grandparents, nay, even to countless living beings, not to mention your own husband, whom you hold most dear. (WND, 533)

The blessings gained by practicing the correct teaching, however, are so great that by meeting minor sufferings in this life we can change the karma

Reflections

BEHAVIOR

"It is when the fruits of studying the Gosho show in our own behavior that we can say we have truly read it."

—Daisaku Ikeda

that destines us to suffer terribly in the future. (WND, 497)

When one carries out the single practice of exercising faith in Myoho-renge-kyo, there are no blessings that fail to come to one, and no good karma that does not begin to work on one's behalf. It is like the case of a fishing net: though the net is composed of innumerable small meshes, when one pulls on the main cord of the net, there are no meshes that do not move. (WND, 133)

BODHISATTVAS

The function of fire is to burn and give light. The function of water is to wash away filth. The winds blow away dust and breathe life into plants, animals, and human beings. The earth produces the grasses and trees, and heaven provides nourishing moisture. The five characters of Myoho-renge-kyo are also like that. They are the cluster of blessings brought by the Bodhisattvas of the Earth, disciples of the Buddha in his true identity. (WND, 218)

The sutra describes the bodhisattvas who emerged from the earth, numerous as the dust particles of a thousand worlds, and who declared, "We ourselves wish to gain this great Law, true and pure." Thus the world of bodhisattvas contains the Ten Worlds. (WND, 357)

Now, no matter what, strive in faith and be known as a votary of the Lotus Sutra, and remain my disciple

Fast Facts

EMERGING FROM THE EARTH

The Bodhisattvas of the Earth appear in the fifteenth chapter of the Lotus Sutra and propagate the teachings of the Mystic Law. They "emerge from the earth," symbolizing the great human potential for wisdom and happiness emerging from within the depths of life—also called the life state of Buddhahood. Those ordinary people who embrace and teach the Mystic Law are the Bodhisattvas of the Earth.

for the rest of your life. If you are of the same mind as Nichiren, you must be a Bodhisattva of the Earth. And if you are a Bodhisattva of the Earth, there is not the slightest doubt that you have been a disciple of Shakyamuni Buddha from the remote past. (WND, 385)

Shakyamuni Buddha refused to entrust the mission of propagation to any of these people and gave it instead to the Bodhisattvas of the Earth. Thus these bodhisattvas are the ones who had thoroughly forged their resolve. (WND, 953)

What then are these two elements of reality and wisdom? They are simply the five characters of Nammyoho-renge-kyo. Shakyamuni Buddha called forth the Bodhisattvas of the Earth and entrusted to them these five characters that constitute the essence of the sutra. This is the teaching that was transferred to the bodhisattvas who had been the disciples of the Buddha since the remote past. (WND, 746)

BUDDHAHOOD

T'ien-t'ai established that the attainment of Buddhahood by persons of the two vehicles is proof that all living beings without exception can become Buddhas. (WND, 58)

A waterfall called the Dragon Gate exists in China. Its waters plunge a hundred feet, swifter than an arrow shot by a strong warrior. It is said that a great many carp gather in the basin below, hoping to climb the falls, and that any that succeeds will turn into a dragon. Not a single carp, however, out of a hundred, a thousand, or even ten thousand, can climb the falls, not even after ten or twenty years. Some are swept away by the strong currents, some fall prey to eagles, hawks, kites, and owls, and others are netted, scooped up, or even shot with arrows by fishermen who line both banks of the falls ten *cho* wide. Such is the difficulty a carp faces in becoming a dragon. . . . Attaining Buddhahood is no easier than for men of low status to enter court circles, or for carp to climb the Dragon Gate. (WND, 1002)

"[At all times I think to myself]: How can I cause living beings to gain entry into the unsurpassed way?" These words express the Buddha's deepest wish to enable both those who accept the Lotus Sutra and those who oppose it to attain Buddhahood. Because this is his ultimate purpose, those who embrace the Lotus Sutra for even a short while are acting in accordance with his will. And if they act in accordance with the Buddha's will, they will be repaying the debt of gratitude they owe to the Buddha. (WND, 63)

To believe that Buddhahood exists within the human world is the most difficult thing of all—as difficult as believing that fire exists in water or water in fire. Nevertheless, the dragon is said to produce fire from water and water from fire, and although people do not understand why, they believe it when they see it occur. Since you now believe that the human world contains the other eight worlds, why are you still unable to include the world of Buddhahood? (WND, 359)

Abutsu-bo is therefore the treasure tower itself, and the treasure tower is Abutsu-bo himself. No other knowledge is purposeful. . . . You may think you offered gifts to the treasure tower of the Thus Come One Many Treasures, but that is not so. You offered them to yourself. (WND, 299)

In the case of the Lotus Sutra, even though people may not have faith in it, so long as they do not slander it, then once they have heard it, they will attain Buddhahood, strange as it may seem. (WND, 513)

Now in the Latter Day of the Law, any person—whether wise or ignorant, priest or lay believer, or of high or low position—who embraces Myoho-renge-kyo and practices it in accordance with the Buddha's teaching, cannot fail to gain the fruit of Buddhahood. (WND, 482)

Shakyamuni, Many Treasures, and the Buddhas of the ten directions represent the world of Buddhahood within ourselves. By searching them out within us, we can receive the benefits of all these Buddhas. (WND, 365)

When we revere Myoho-renge-kyo inherent in our own life as the object of

People to Know

SHAKYAMUNI

As a young man, Shakyamuni was not content with his princely life. He left the palace he grew up in and set out to answer life's fundamental questions. He eventually awakened to the fact that all human beings have the seed for Buddhahood. He dedicated the remainder of his life to teaching how all people could uncover their innate wisdom.

devotion, the Buddha nature within us is summoned forth and manifested by our chanting of Nam-myoho-renge-kyo. This is what is meant by "Buddha." To illustrate, when a caged bird sings, birds who are flying in the sky are thereby summoned and gather around, and when the birds flying in the sky gather around, the bird in the cage strives to get out. When with our mouths we chant the Mystic Law, our Buddha nature, being summoned, will invariably emerge. (WND, 887)

The Lotus Sutra is the king of sutras, the direct path to enlightenment, for it explains that the entity of our life, which manifests either good or evil at each moment, is in fact the entity of the Mystic Law. If you chant Myoho-renge-kyo with deep faith in this principle, you are certain to attain Buddhahood in this lifetime. (WND, 4)

When he was alive, he was a Buddha in life, and now he is a Buddha in death. He is a Buddha in both life and death. This is what is meant by that most important doctrine called attaining Buddhahood in one's present form. (WND, 456)

We ordinary beings are fettered by evil karma, earthly desires, and the sufferings of birth and death. But due to the three inherent potentials of the Buddha nature—innate Buddhahood, the wisdom to perceive it, and the actions to manifest it—we can without doubt reveal the Buddha's three bodies—the Dharma body, the reward body, and the manifested body. (WND, 923)

Just as a commoner can become a king in this present life, so can an ordinary person become a Buddha instantly. This is the heart of the doctrine of three thousand realms in a single moment of life. (WND, 324)

Reflections

NEVER BECOMING DEADLOCKED

"As long as we continue to study the Gosho and put its teachings into practice, we definitely will never become deadlocked." —Daisaku Ikeda

There are trails in the sky where birds fly, but people cannot recognize them. There are paths in the sea along which fish swim, but people cannot perceive them. . . .

But they are visible to the heavenly eye. In like manner, ordinary people cannot see that the "Treasure Tower" chapter exists within the body of Nichinyo, but Shakyamuni, Many Treasures, and the Buddhas of the ten directions perceive it. I, Nichiren, also presume this to be the case. (WND, 915–16)

Nichiren poured his life into writing letters
to encourage his followers.

CARE FOR OTHERS

Toki has told me that, while grieved at his mother's death, he was grateful that she passed away peacefully, and that you gave her such attentive care. He said joyfully that he would never be able to forget this in any lifetime to come. (WND, 656)

Nevertheless, despite all the risks involved, you traveled to Sado carrying your infant daughter, since her father, from whom you have long been separated, was not to be depended upon for her care. I cannot even imagine the hardships you must have suffered during your journey, much less describe them in words, so I will lay down my writing brush. (WND, 325)

To such a place, where friends from former times never come to visit, where I have been abandoned even by my own disciples, you have sent these vessels, which I heap with snow, imagining it to be rice, and from which I drink water, thinking it to be gruel. Please let your thoughts dwell on the effects of your kindness. There is much more I would like to say. (WND, 1022)

Because I care about you, I have written this letter as a guide. I hope you will study it when you have time. (WND, 868)

It is easy to sustain our concern for someone who is before our very eyes, but quite a different thing when that person is far away, even though in our heart we may not forget him. Nevertheless, in the five years . . . that have already passed since I came to live here in the mountains, you have sent your husband from the province of Sado to visit me three times. How great is your sincerity! It is firmer than the great earth, deeper than the great sea! (WND, 933)

The lay priest who bears this letter tells me that you instructed him to accompany me to the province of Sado. But in view of the expenses of the trip and other difficulties, I am sending him back to you. I already know the depths of your consideration. Please explain to the others what I have written here. I am very much concerned about the priests who are in prison, and I hope you will inform me of their situation at your earliest convenience. (WND, 210)

CAUSE AND EFFECT

What one has done for another yesterday will be done for oneself today. Blossoms turn into fruit, and brides become mothers-in-law. Chant Nam-myoho-renge-kyo, and be always diligent in your faith. (WND, 994)

The Buddha taught that one, from the very moment of one's birth, is accompanied by two messengers, Same Birth and Same Name, who are sent by heaven and who follow one as closely as one's own shadow, never parting from one even for an instant. These two take turns ascending to heaven to report one's offenses and good deeds, both great and small, without overlooking the slightest detail. Therefore, heaven too must know about this matter. How reassuring! How reassuring! (WND, 316)

Just as flowers open up and bear fruit, just as the moon appears and invariably grows full, just as a lamp becomes brighter when oil is added, and just as plants and trees flourish with rain, so will human beings never fail to prosper when they make good causes. (WND, 1013)

The benefit of all the other sutras is uncertain, because they teach that one must first make good causes and only then can one become a Buddha at some later time. With regard to the Lotus Sutra, when one's hand takes it up, that hand immediately attains Buddhahood, and when one's mouth chants it, that mouth is itself a Buddha, as, for example, the moon is reflected in the water the moment it appears from behind the eastern mountains, or as a sound and its echo arise simultaneously. (WND, 1099)

Reflections

INEXTINGUISHABLE SUN

"The harder the times I faced, the more eagerly I sought the Daishonin's words. And each time that I did, I found new courage. An inextinguishable sun rose in my heart, breaking through the darkness."
—Daisaku Ikeda

Whether you chant the Buddha's name, recite the sutra, or merely offer flowers and incense, all your virtuous acts will implant benefits and roots of goodness in your life. With this conviction you should strive in faith. (WND, 4)

When I hold up the bright mirror of the Lotus Sutra before me, all is crystal-clear; there can be no doubt that in my previous existences I was guilty of slandering the Law. If in my present existence I do not wipe out that offense, then in the future how can I escape the pains of hell? (WND, 436)

"One scholar enumerates the types of evil as follows: 'I will first list the evil causes and then their effects. There are fourteen evil causes: (1) arrogance, (2) negligence, (3) wrong views of the self, (4) shallow understanding, (5) attachment to earthly desires, (6) not understanding, (7) not believing, (8) scowling with knitted brows, (9) harboring doubts, (10) slandering, (11) despising, (12) hating, (13) envying, and (14) bearing grudges.'" Since these fourteen slanders apply equally to priesthood and laity, you must be on guard against them. (WND, 756)

CHARACTER

A good believer is one who does not depend upon persons of eminence or despise those of humble station; who does not rely on the backing of superiors or look down on inferiors; who, not relying upon the opinions of others, upholds the Lotus Sutra among all the sutras. Such a person the Buddha has called the best of all people. (WND, 880)

The number of those endowed with human life is as small as the amount of earth one can place on a fingernail. Life as a human being is hard to sustain—as hard as it is for the dew to remain on the grass. But it is better to live a single day with honor than to live to 120 and die in disgrace. Live so that all the people of Kamakura will say in your praise that Nakatsukasa Saburo Saemon-no-jo is diligent in the service of his lord, in the service of Buddhism, and in his concern for other people. (WND, 851)

Do not go around lamenting to others how hard it is for you to live in this world. To do so is an act utterly unbecoming to a worthy man. (WND, 850)

Mugwort that grows in the midst of hemp, or a snake inside a tube [will as a matter of course become straight], and those who associate with people of good character will consequently become upright in heart, deed, and word. The Lotus Sutra exerts a similar influence. The Buddha will look upon one who simply puts faith in this sutra as a good person. (WND, 1128)

CHILDREN

Even animals of little intelligence cannot endure parting from their young. The golden pheasant at Bamboo Grove Monastery plunged into flames and

During their infant daughter's illness, Shijo Kingo and
Nichigen-nyo gained inspiration from Nichiren's letter.

died to save her eggs. The stag at Deer Park offered himself to the king to save a female deer's unborn fawn. How much greater, then, must be the love of human beings toward their children! (WND, 662)

Tsukimaro must have chanted Nam-myoho-renge-kyo with her very first cry at birth. The Lotus Sutra speaks of "the true aspect of all phenomena." T'ien-t'ai said, "Voices do the Buddha's work." This is also what I think. The deaf cannot hear the thunder, and the blind cannot see the light of the sun and moon. But I am quite certain that the ten demon daughters must be together side by side, giving the baby her first bath and watching over her growth. (WND, 188)

A woman called Shodai-nyo, for the faults of greed and stinginess, was confined in the realm of hungry spirits, but she was saved by her son Maudgalyayana and was freed from that realm. Thus the sutra's statement that children are a treasure is in no way false. (WND, 1091)

The service for deceased ancestors has its origins in the events arising from the Venerable Maudgalyayana's attempts to save his mother, Shodai-nyo, who, because of her karma of greed and stinginess, had fallen into the world of hungry spirits for a period of five hundred lifetimes. He failed, however, to make his mother a Buddha. The reason was that he himself was not yet a votary of the Lotus Sutra, and so he could not lead even his mother to Buddhahood. At the eight-year assembly on Eagle Peak, he embraced the Lotus Sutra and chanted Nam-myoho-renge-kyo, and became Tamalapattra Sandalwood Fragrance Buddha. At this time, his mother also became a Buddha. (WND, 190)

COMMON SENSE

Determine to take every possible precaution. Those who hate you will be increasingly vigilant in watching for a chance to do you harm. Put a stop to all drinking parties at night. What dissatisfaction can there be in drinking sake alone with your wife? Do not let down your guard when you attend banquets with others in the daytime. Your enemies will have no opportunity to attack you, apart from your drinking. You cannot be too careful. (WND, 461)

Buddhism is reason. Reason will win over your lord. No matter how dearly you may love your wife and wish never to part from her, when you die, it will be to no avail. No matter how dearly you may cherish your estate, when you die, it will only fall into the hands of others. You have been prosperous enough for all these years. You must not give your estate a second thought. As I have said before, be millions of times more careful than ever. (WND, 839)

When you have something urgent to tell me, send a messenger. Indeed, I was deeply worried about your last trip. An enemy will try to make you forget the danger so that he can attack. If you should have to travel, do not begrudge the cost of a horse. Make sure that you ride a good horse. Bring along your best men to defend you against a surprise attack, and ride a horse that can easily carry you in your armor. (WND, 952–53)

COMPASSION

When it comes to understanding the Lotus Sutra, I have only a minute fraction of the vast ability that T'ien-t'ai and Dengyo possessed. But as regards my ability to endure persecution and the wealth of my compassion for others, I believe they would hold me in awe. (WND, 242)

Utsubusa came a long distance to visit me despite her advanced age, but since I was told that it was merely a casual visit on her

People to Know

T'IEN-T'AI, MIAO-LO AND DENGYO

Three men are credited for spreading the Lotus Sutra throughout East Asia: T'ien-t'ai, Miao-lo and Dengyo. T'ien-t'ai founded the Chinese Buddhist school that upheld the Lotus Sutra as Shakyamuni's highest teaching by classifying all of the Buddhist sutras. Miao-lo, revered as a restorer of the T'ien-t'ai school, wrote invaluable commentaries. Dengyo followed in the T'ien-t'ai tradition in Japan and laid the groundwork for Nichiren's emergence in the thirteenth century.

way back from the shrine to the god of her ancestors, I would not see her, although I pitied her greatly. Had I permitted her to see me, I would have been allowing her to commit slander against the

Lotus Sutra. The reason is that all gods are subjects, and the Lotus Sutra is their lord. It is against even the code of society to visit one's lord on the way back from calling on one of his subjects. . . . Utsubusa is the same age that my parents would be. I feel deeply sorry to have disappointed her, but I want her to understand this point. (WND, 896)

The words of the sutra, which are as full of compassion as a mother's love, will then find solace, and the cares of the Buddha, who said, "I am the only person who can rescue and protect others," will likewise be eased. (WND, 63)

But it is not enough that I alone should accept and have faith in your words—we must see to it that others as well are warned of their errors. (WND, 26)

It is said that even the moonlight will not deign to shine on the sleeve of an unfeeling person. (WND, 62)

CONVICTION

My resolution is now immovable. Determined to endure any hardship, I have fulfilled the Buddha's prediction, and I have not the slightest doubt. (WND, 895)

It seems to me that on the path to attain Buddhahood it may invariably be when one has done something like lay down one's life that one becomes a Buddha. I think that perhaps it is encountering such difficulties as have already been explained in the sutra—being cursed, vilified, attacked with swords and staves, shards and rubble, and banished again and again—that is reading the Lotus Sutra with one's life. My faith springs up all the more, and I am confident about my next existence. (WND, 202)

You, yourself, are a Thus Come One who is originally enlightened and endowed with the three bodies. You should chant Nam-myoho-renge-kyo with this conviction. Then the place where you chant daimoku will become the dwelling place of the treasure tower. (WND, 299–300)

Today there are people who have faith in the Lotus Sutra. The belief of some is like fire while that of others is like water. When the former listen to the teachings, their passion flares up like fire, but as time goes on, they tend to discard their faith. To have faith like water means to believe continuously without ever regressing. (WND, 899)

Concerning the ways of the ordinary world, though a man may not be inclined to a certain act, if he is urged to it by his parents, his sovereign, his teachers, his wife and children, or his close friends, and if he is a person of conscience, he will overlook his own inclinations and will sacrifice his name and profit, and even his life, to perform that act. How much more earnest will he be, then, if the act is something that springs from his own heart. In such a case, even the restraints of his parents, his sovereign, or his teachers cannot prevent him from carrying out the action. (WND, 340–41)

The mighty warrior General Li Kuang, whose mother had been devoured by a tiger, shot an arrow at the stone he believed was the tiger. The arrow penetrated the stone all the way up to its feathers. But once he realized it was only a stone, he was unable to pierce it again. Later he came to be known as General Stone Tiger. This story applies to you. Though enemies lurk in wait for you, your resolute faith in the Lotus Sutra has forestalled great dangers before they could begin. Realizing this, you must strengthen your faith more than ever. (WND, 953)

People to Know

NANJO TOKIMITSU

After his father and elder brother died, Nanjo Tokimitsu was forced to take on the responsibilities as steward of Ueno Village while still in his teens. He took faith in Nichiren's teachings and supported many of Nichiren's followers during the Atsuhara Persecution. He sheltered some in his home and used his influence to negotiate the release of others who were imprisoned.

Since I willingly bring these troubles upon myself, when others vilify me, I do not rebuke them. Even if I wanted to rebuke them, there are too many of them. And even when they strike me, I feel no pain, for I have been prepared for their blows from the very beginning. (WND, 728)

This I will state. Let the gods forsake me. Let all persecutions assail me. Still I will give my life for the sake of the Law. (WND, 280)

COURAGE

The heart of strategy and swordsmanship derives from the Mystic Law. Have profound faith. A coward cannot have any of his prayers answered. (WND, 1001)

In commenting on this passage, I have this to say: Shakyamuni taught that the shallow is easy to embrace, but the profound is difficult. To discard the shallow and seek the profound is the way of a person of courage. (WND, 558)

You should not have the slightest fear in your heart. It is lack of courage that prevents one from attaining Buddhahood, although one may have professed faith in the Lotus Sutra many times since innumerable kalpas ago. (WND, 637)

None of you who declare yourselves to be my disciples should ever give way to cowardice. (WND, 764)

Each of you should summon up the courage of a lion king and never succumb to threats from anyone. The lion king fears no other beast, nor do its cubs. Slanderers are like barking foxes, but Nichiren's followers are like roaring lions. (WND, 997)

A sword is useless in the hands of a coward. The mighty sword of the Lotus Sutra must be wielded by one courageous in faith. Then one will be as strong as a demon armed with an iron staff. (WND, 412)

Harsh weather never deterred Abutsu-bo from bringing
offerings to Nichiren on Mount Minobu.

Thus it seemed that I could not possibly escape with my life. Whatever the design of the heavenly gods in the matter may have been, every single steward and Nembutsu believer worthy of the name kept strict watch on my hut day and night, determined to prevent anyone from communicating with me. Never in any lifetime will I forget how in those circumstances you, with Abutsu-bo carrying a wooden container of food on his back, came in the night again and again to bring me aid. (WND, 932–33)

A brilliant orb as bright as the moon burst forth from the direction of Enoshima, shooting across the sky from southeast to northwest. It was shortly before dawn and still too dark to see anyone's face, but the radiant object clearly illuminated everyone like bright moonlight. The executioner fell on his face, his eyes blinded. The soldiers were filled with panic. Some ran off into the distance, some jumped down from their horses and huddled on the ground, while others crouched in their saddles. I called out, "Here, why do you shrink from this vile prisoner? Come closer! Come closer!" But no one would approach me. (WND, 767)

DEATH

For one who summons up one's faith and chants Nam-myoho-renge-kyo with the profound insight that now is the last moment of one's life, the sutra proclaims: "When the lives of these persons come to an end, they will be received into the hands of a thousand Buddhas, who will free them from all fear and keep them from falling into the evil paths of existence." (WND, 216)

The companions with whom we enjoyed composing poems praising the moon on autumn evenings have vanished with the moon behind the shifting clouds. Only their mute images remain in our hearts. Though the moon has set behind the western mountains, we will compose poetry under it again next autumn. But where are our companions who have passed away? Even when the approaching tiger of death roars, we do not hear and are not startled. How many more days are left to the sheep bound for slaughter? (WND, 1027)

Be resolved to summon forth the great power of faith, and chant Nam-myoho-renge-kyo with the prayer that your faith will be steadfast and correct at the moment of death. Never seek any other way to inherit the ultimate Law of life and death, and manifest it in your life. Only then will you realize that earthly desires are

Reflections

SURMOUNTING OBSTACLES

If you uphold the Gosho
Overflowing with the power
  of the Buddha
The strength to surmount
  every obstacle
Will arise within you.
  —Josei Toda

enlightenment, and that the sufferings of birth and death are nirvana. Even embracing the Lotus Sutra would be useless without the heritage of faith. (WND, 218)

Though you may move among the most exalted company of court nobles, your hair done up elegantly like clouds and your sleeves fluttering like eddies of snow, such pleasures, when you stop to consider them, are no more than a dream within a dream. You must come to rest at last under the carpet of weeds at the foot of the hill, and all your jeweled daisies and brocade hangings will mean nothing to you on the road to the afterlife. (WND, 106)

The spring blossoms depart with the wind; maple leaves turn red in autumn showers. All are proof that no living thing can stay for long in this world. Therefore, the Lotus Sutra counsels us, "Nothing in this world is lasting or firm but all are like bubbles, foam, heat shimmer." (WND, 63)

Those who have become the disciples and lay supporters of such a Nichiren—especially your deceased mother, Myoho, the anniversary of whose death falls on the twelfth day of this month—are votaries of the

Lotus Sutra and my lay supporters. How could she possibly have fallen into the world of hungry spirits? No doubt she is now in the presence of Shakyamuni Buddha, Many Treasures Buddha, and the Buddhas of the ten directions. (WND, 191)

In the end, no one can escape death. The sufferings at that time will be exactly like what we are experiencing now. Since death is the same in either case, you should be willing to offer your life for the Lotus Sutra. Think of this offering as a drop of dew rejoining the ocean, or a speck of dust returning to the earth. (WND, 1003)

As I have been saying for some time, in your situation as a lay believer, you should just single-mindedly chant Nam-myoho-renge-kyo morning and evening, day and night, and observe what happens at the last moments of your life. At that time, hasten to the summit of perfect enlightenment, and look around you in all directions. The entire realm of phenomena will have changed into the Land of Tranquil Light . . . Buddhas and bodhisattvas all being caressed by breezes of eternity, happiness, true self, and purity. We, too, will surely be among their number. (WND, 843)

No matter what, always keep your faith in the Lotus Sutra steadfast. Then, at the last moment of your life, you will be welcomed by a thousand Buddhas, who will take you swiftly to the pure land of Eagle Peak where you will experience the boundless joy of the Law. (WND, 1030)

Nam-myoho-renge-kyo will be your staff to take you safely over the mountains of death. The Buddhas Shakyamuni and Many Treasures, as well as the four bodhisattvas headed by Superior Practices, will lead you by the hand on your journey. If I, Nichiren, precede you in death, I will come to meet you at your last moment. If you should precede me, I will be sure to tell King Yama all about you. Everything that I tell you is true. According to the Lotus Sutra, Nichiren is the guide who knows the passes and gorges along the way. (WND, 451–52)

DEBT OF GRATITUDE

All these things I have done solely to repay the debt I owe to my parents, the debt I owe to my teacher, the debt I owe to the three treasures of Buddhism, and the debt I owe to my country. For their sake I have been willing to destroy my body and to give up my life, though as it turns out, I have not been put to death after all. (WND, 728)

Even lowly creatures know enough to repay a debt of gratitude. Thus the bird known as the wild goose will invariably carry out its filial duty to the mother bird when she is about to die. And the fox never forgets its old hillock. If even animals will do such things, then how much more so should this be true of human beings? (WND, 337)

If a worthy man makes three attempts to warn the rulers of the nation and they still refuse to heed his advice, then he should retire to a mountain forest. This has been the custom from ages past, and I have accordingly followed it. I am quite certain that the merit I have acquired through my efforts is recognized by everyone from the three treasures on down to Brahma, Shakra, and the gods of the sun and moon. Through this merit I will surely lead to enlightenment my parents and my teacher, the late Dozen-bo. (WND, 728)

People to Know

DOZEN-BO

Dozen-bo was Nichiren's teacher when he entered Seicho-ji temple at age 12. Years later, Nichiren taught Nam-myoho-renge-kyo there. His declaration angered the local steward, who soon sent men to kill him. Taking pity on his former student, Dozen-bo helped Nichiren escape. Nichiren continued to share the Lotus Sutra with him, never forgetting his debt of gratitude.

All these different species of beings brought flowers, incense, clothing, and food as their last offerings to the Buddha. . . . Not only did their tears flow, but they beat their heads, pressed their hands to their chests, and cried aloud, not sparing their voices. The blood of their tears and the blood of their sweat fell upon Kushinagara more heavily than a torrential rain and flowed more abundantly than a mighty river. All this they did solely because the Lotus Sutra had opened for them the way to Buddhahood, and they could never repay the debt of gratitude they owed the Buddha. (WND, 345)

Concerning the debt owed to the Law, the Law is the teacher of all Buddhas. It is because of the Law that the Buddhas are worthy of respect. Therefore, those who wish to repay their debt to the Buddha must first repay the debt they owe to the Law. (WND, 44)

One who studies the teachings of Buddhism must not fail to repay the four debts of gratitude. According to the Contemplation on the Mind-Ground Sutra, the first of the four debts is that owed to all living beings. Were it not for them, one would find it impossible to make the vow to save innumerable living beings. Moreover, but for the evil people who persecute bodhisattvas, how could those bodhisattvas increase their merit? (WND, 43)

People to Know

NIIKE

It wasn't easy for government officials to declare themselves a follower of Nichiren. Doing so often meant censure, ridicule or other forms of persecution. Still, Niike Saemon-no-jo and his wife, the lay nun Niike, heard about Nichiren's teachings through Nikko. They decided to put their trust in Nichiren, and later Niike travelled with Nikko to see Nichiren at his dwelling on Mount Minobu.

Thus those people who slandered me and the ruler [who had me banished] are the very persons to whom I owe the most profound debt of gratitude. (WND, 43)

Even if we should gather all the water of the four great oceans to wet inkstones, burn all the trees and plants to make ink sticks, collect the hairs of all

beasts for writing brushes, employ all the surfaces of
the worlds in the ten directions for paper, and, with
these, set down expressions of gratitude, how could
we possibly repay our debt to the Buddha? (WND, 44)

The Buddha taught that the blessings of a single
offering to the votary of this sutra are a hundred,
thousand, ten thousand, million times greater than
those of offering countless treasures to Shakyamuni
Buddha for eighty million kalpas. When one encounters this sutra, one will overflow with happiness and
shed tears of joy. (WND, 1027)

Ever since I began to study the Law handed down
from Shakyamuni Buddha and undertook the practice of the Buddhist teachings, I have believed it is
most important to understand one's obligations to
others, and made it my first duty to repay such debts
of kindness. In this world, we owe four debts of gratitude. One who understands this is worthy to be
called human, while one who does not is no more
than an animal. (WND, 122)

DEVOTION

I learned that the scholar Nichigen of Jisso-ji temple,
upon becoming my disciple, was driven out by his
own disciples and lay supporters, and had to give up
his lands, so that he now has no place of his own.
Nonetheless, he still visits me and takes care of
my disciples. What devotion to the way! Nichigen is
a sage. He is already unrivaled as a scholar of

Buddhism. Yet he has discarded all desire for fame and fortune and become my disciple. (WND, 755)

In accordance with this passage, Nichiren, as this bodhisattva's envoy, has urged the people of Japan to accept and uphold the Lotus Sutra. His unremitting efforts never slacken, even here on this mountain. (WND, 993)

Bring forth the great power of faith, and be spoken of by all the people of Kamakura, both high and low, or by all the people of Japan, as "Shijo Kingo, Shijo Kingo of the Lotus school!" Even a bad reputation will spread far and wide. A good reputation will spread even farther, particularly if it is a reputation for devotion to the Lotus Sutra. (WND, 319)

Now when I consider the sincere offerings that you have sent, I think that, though the late Nanjo undoubtedly loved you dearly as his son, he probably never imagined that you would in this way, through the Lotus Sutra, discharge your filial duty to him. Even if he was perhaps guilty of some offense, no matter where he may be now, your filial devotion will surely be recognized even by King Yama and the heavenly kings Brahma and Shakra. And how could Shakyamuni Buddha and the Lotus Sutra ever abandon him? Your devotion is no less than that of that young boy who untied his father's bonds. I am writing this through my tears. (WND, 678)

I, Nichiren, am the richest man in all of present-day Japan. I have dedicated my life to the Lotus Sutra, and my name will be handed down in ages to come. (WND, 268)

No matter what grave offenses you might have committed, because you did not turn against the Lotus Sutra, but showed your devotion by accompanying me, you will surely become a Buddha. . . . Faith in the Lotus Sutra acts as a prayer [to attain Buddhahood]. Strengthen your resolve to seek the way all the more and achieve Buddhahood in this lifetime. (WND, 946)

DIVERSITY

People have varied tastes. Some prefer good and some prefer evil. There are many kinds of people. But though they differ from one another in such ways, once they enter into the Lotus Sutra, they all become like a single person in body and a single person in mind. This is just like the myriad different rivers that, when they flow into the ocean, all take on a uniformly salty flavor, or like the many kinds of birds that, when they approach Mount Sumeru, all assume the same [golden] hue. (WND, 1042)

Cherry, plum, peach or damson blossoms—all, just as they are, are entities possessing their own unique qualities. (GZ, 784)

There should be no discrimination among those who propagate the five characters of Myoho-renge-kyo in the Latter Day of the Law, be they men or women. Were they not Bodhisattvas of the Earth, they could not chant the daimoku. (WND, 385)

DOUBT

If you do not question and resolve your doubts, you cannot dispel the dark clouds of illusion, any more than you could travel a thousand miles without legs. (WND, 1031)

If people should try to weaken your belief in the Lotus Sutra, consider that your faith is being tested. (WND, 800)

Even a heartless villain loves his wife and children. He too has a portion of the bodhisattva world within him. Buddhahood is the most difficult to demonstrate. But since you possess the other nine worlds, you should believe that you have Buddhahood as well. Do not permit yourself to have doubts. (WND, 358)

Suppose there is a ship that sails on the open sea. Though the ship is stoutly built, if it is flooded by a leak, those on the ship are sure to drown together. Though the embankment between rice fields is firm, if there is an ant hole in it, then surely, in the long run, it will not remain full of water. Bail the seawater of slander and disbelief out of the ship of your life, and solidify the embankments of your faith. (WND, 626)

According to Acharya Ben, you said to him: "I have been practicing the Lotus Sutra correctly since last year, when you told me that those who embrace this sutra will 'enjoy peace and security in their present existence and good circumstances in future existences.' Instead, however, great hardships have showered down on me like rain." Is this true, or did he give me a false report? In either case, I will take advantage of this opportunity to resolve any doubts you may have. (WND, 471)

One who holds me in contempt and does not chant Nam-myoho-renge-kyo is like a baby who doubts its mother's milk and refuses the breast, or a sick man who is suspicious of his physician and rejects the medicine prescribed for him. (WND, 861)

Suppose that a person is standing at the foot of a tall embankment and is unable to ascend. And suppose that there is someone on top of the embankment who lowers a rope and says, "If you take hold of this rope, I will pull you up to the top of the embankment." If the person at the bottom begins to doubt that the other has the strength to pull him up, or wonders if the rope is not too weak and therefore refuses to put forth his hand and grasp it, then how is he ever to get to the top of the embankment? But if he follows the instructions, puts out his hand, and takes hold of the rope, then he can climb up. (WND, 59)

You must be guided by the intent of [the Lotus Sutra, which is] the immediate attainment of enlightenment, and never give yourself up to the mistaken views that stem from doubts or attachments. (WND, 63)

Because Oama is insincere and foolish, sometimes she believes, but other times she doubts. She is irresolute. When Nichiren incurred the wrath of the government authorities, she discarded the Lotus Sutra. This is what I meant before, when I told her whenever we met that the Lotus Sutra is "the most difficult to believe and the most difficult to understand." (WND, 468)

And yet the people doubt me, and I too have doubts about myself. Why do the gods not assist me? Heavenly gods and other guardian deities made their vow before the Buddha. Even if the votary of the Lotus Sutra were an ape rather than a man, they should address him as the votary of the Lotus Sutra and rush forward to fulfill the vow they made before the Buddha. Does their failure to do so mean that I am in fact not a votary of the Lotus Sutra? This doubt lies at the heart of this piece I am writing. And because it is the most important concern of my entire life, I will raise it again and again here, and emphasize it more than ever, before I attempt to answer it. (WND, 243)

These doubts of yours are most opportune. I will take the occasion to clear up the points that puzzle you. (WND, 278)

Although I and my disciples may encounter various difficulties, if we do not harbor doubts in our hearts, we will as a matter of course attain Buddhahood. Do not have doubts simply because heaven does not lend you protection. Do not be discouraged because you do not enjoy an easy and secure existence in this life. This is what I have taught my disciples morning and evening, and yet they begin to harbor doubts and abandon their faith. (WND, 283)

People to Know

NICHIMYO

Nichimyo traveled from Kamakura to Sado Island to visit Nichiren. She braved extreme weather conditions, treacherous sea travel, lack of food and water, threat of raiders and soldiers—all the while carrying an infant baby on her back. Because of her strong faith, Nichiren gave her the name Sage Nichimyo [Sun Wonderful], indicating that she would become a Buddha.

If one doubts the strength of the Buddha when he says, "I am the only person who can rescue and protect others"; if one is suspicious of the rope held out by the Lotus Sutra when its teachings declare that one can "gain entrance through faith alone"; if one fails to chant the Mystic Law which guarantees that "such a person assuredly and without doubt [will attain the Buddha way]," then the Buddha's power cannot reach one, and it will be impossible to scale the embankment of enlightenment. (WND, 59–60)

Nichiren taught that the way for people to cause the
sun of happiness to rise in their hearts was through
chanting Nam-myoho-renge-kyo.

ENLIGHTENMENT

When one is deluded, it is as if one were dreaming. And when one is enlightened, it is as if one had awakened. (WND, 758)

If Devadatta, who committed three of the five cardinal sins and in addition was guilty of countless other grave offenses, could become the Thus Come One Heavenly King, then there can be no doubt that the other evildoers who committed only one or two of the cardinal sins will surely attain the way as well. For if the great earth itself could be overturned, then the plants and trees on it would as a matter of course be overturned. And if one can crush the hardest stone, one can certainly bend the pliant grasses. (WND, 147)

Devadatta was a man of incorrigible disbelief, the worst in the entire land of Jambudvipa. In all the earlier sutras preached during the lifetime of the Buddha, he was cast aside as hopeless. But he encountered the Lotus Sutra, and was granted a prediction that he would become a Buddha called the Thus Come One Heavenly King. Judging from these examples, we may conclude that for evil people living in the latter age the attainment of Buddhahood depends not upon whether their offenses are slight or grave, but solely upon whether or not they have faith in this sutra. (WND, 409)

Here it is told how the dragon girl became a Buddha in her reptilian form. And at that moment there was no longer anyone who doubted that all men can attain Buddhahood. This is why I say that the enlightenment of women is expounded as a model. (WND, 930)

Rice plants change and become seedlings. Seedlings change and become stalks. Stalks change and become rice. Rice changes and becomes a person. And a person changes and becomes a Buddha. A woman changes and becomes the single character *myo*. The character *myo* changes and becomes Shakyamuni Buddha seated on a lotus pedestal. (WND, 1089)

People can attain enlightenment in two ways: by meeting the Buddha and hearing the Lotus Sutra, or by believing in the sutra even though they do not meet the Buddha. (WND, 359)

The mystic principle that is the essential nature of phenomena possesses two aspects, the defiled aspect and the pure aspect. If the defiled aspect is operative, this is called delusion. If the pure aspect is operative,

---

Fast Facts

SHAKYAMUNI'S AWAKENING

The Ceremony in the Air is one of the three assemblies described in the Lotus Sutra. The heart of the ceremony consists of Shakyamuni revealing the idea of his enlightenment in the remote past, many lifetimes ago, and the transfer of the Lotus Sutra's essence to the Bodhisattvas of the Earth.

---

this is called enlightenment. Enlightenment constitutes the realm of Buddhahood. Delusion constitutes the realms of ordinary mortals. (WND, 417)

EQUALITY

In the Latter Day of the Law, no treasure tower exists other than the figures of the men and women who embrace the Lotus Sutra. It follows, therefore, that whether eminent or humble, high or low, those who chant Nam-myoho-renge-kyo are themselves the treasure tower, and, likewise, are themselves the Thus Come One Many Treasures. (WND, 299)

The Buddha surely considers anyone in this world who embraces the Lotus Sutra, whether lay man or woman, monk or nun, to be the lord of all living beings, and Brahma and Shakra most certainly hold that person in reverence. When I think in this way, my joy is beyond expression. (WND, 463)

Bound as we common mortals are by earthly desires, we can instantly attain the same virtues as Shakyamuni Buddha, for we receive all the benefits that he accumulated. The sutra reads, "Hoping to make all persons equal to me, without any distinction between us." This means that those who believe in and practice the Lotus Sutra are equal to Shakyamuni Buddha. (WND, 323)

Shakyamuni Buddha who attained enlightenment countless kalpas ago, the Lotus Sutra that leads all people to Buddhahood, and we ordinary human beings are in no way different or separate from one another. To chant Myoho-renge-kyo with this realization is to inherit the ultimate Law of life and death. This is a matter of the utmost importance for Nichiren's disciples and lay supporters, and this is what it means to embrace the Lotus Sutra. (WND, 216)

Faith in Daily Life

WE'RE ALL EQUAL

Nichiren emphasized the innate equality of all people. He often pointed out that there is no distinction between the Buddha, the Lotus Sutra and ordinary people who uphold this teaching. This revolutionary idea caused quite a stir among priests of other sects, who considered themselves to be of special status. Nichiren's teaching of equality makes it clear that nothing can stand between us, the Mystic Law and ultimately our happiness.

All those who keep faith in the Lotus Sutra are most certainly Buddhas, and one who slanders a Buddha commits a grave offense. When one chants the daimoku bearing in mind that there are no distinctions among those who embrace the Lotus Sutra, then the blessings one gains will be equal to those of Shakyamuni Buddha. (WND, 756)

Even an ignorant person can obtain blessings by serving someone who expounds the Lotus Sutra. No matter if he is a demon or an animal, if someone proclaims even a single verse or phrase of the Lotus Sutra, you must respect him as you would the

Buddha. This is what the sutra means when it says, "You should rise and greet him from afar, showing him the same respect you would a Buddha." You should respect one another as Shakyamuni and Many Treasures did at the ceremony in the "Treasure Tower" chapter. (WND, 757)

ETERNITY OF LIFE

How wonderful then is your having wholeheartedly supported the votary of the Lotus Sutra over the years! According to the Buddha's golden words, in the next life you are certain to be reborn in the pure land of Eagle Peak. What remarkable rewards you will gain! (WND, 1097)

From the time that I was born until today, I have never known a moment's ease; I have thought only of propagating the daimoku of the Lotus Sutra. I do not know how long I or anyone else may live, but without fail, I will be with you at the time of your death and guide you from this life to the next. (WND, 965)

Though this mandala has but five or seven characters, it is the teacher of all Buddhas throughout the three existences and the seal that guarantees the enlightenment of all women. It will be a lamp in the darkness of the road to the next world and a fine horse to carry you over the mountains of death. It is like the sun and moon in the heavens or Mount Sumeru on earth. It is a ship to ferry people over the sea of the sufferings of birth and death. It is the teacher who leads all people to Buddhahood and enlightenment. (WND, 414)

The Lotus Sutra is the robe that will keep you from disgrace after this life. The sutra reads, "It is like a robe to one who is naked." Believe in the Gohonzon with all your heart, for it is the robe to protect you in the world after death. (WND, 994)

We living beings, right down to crickets, ants, mosquitoes, and flies, all possess life that is without beginning or end. (GZ, 382)

FAITH

The strong and steadfast power of faith is precious indeed. (WND, 197)

I have found that even those who appear to believe just as the sutra teaches may not actually have strong faith at all, as you are already well aware. . . . The fact that her prayers have gone unanswered is like a strong bow with a weak bowstring, or a fine sword in the hands of a coward. It is in no sense the fault of the Lotus Sutra. (WND, 489)

Make every possible effort for the sake of your next life. What is most important is that, by chanting Nam-myoho-renge-kyo alone, you can attain Buddhahood. It will no doubt depend on the strength of your faith. To have faith is the basis of Buddhism. Thus the fourth volume of *Great Concentration and Insight* states,

People to Know

NICHIGEN-NYO

Nichigen-nyo allowed her husband, Shijo Kingo, to make the treacherous journey to visit the Daishonin on Sado Island. Knowing full well the dangers involved, and the risks of not having him there to protect her and her daughter, she put her entire faith in the Lotus Sutra, living courageously and praying for his safe return.

"Buddhism is like an ocean that one can only enter with faith." (WND, 832)

I cannot see the sun in the daytime or the moon at night. In winter there is deep snow, and in summer the grass grows thick. Because so few people come to see me, the trail is very hard to travel. This year, especially, the snow is so deep that I have no visitors at all. Knowing that my life may end at any time, I put all my trust in the Lotus Sutra. (WND, 779)

Suffer what there is to suffer, enjoy what there is to enjoy. Regard both suffering and joy as facts of life, and continue chanting Nam-myoho-renge-kyo, no matter what happens. How could this be anything other than the boundless joy of the Law? Strengthen your power of faith more than ever. (WND, 681)

He states, however, that if a woman's faith is weak, even though she embraces the Lotus Sutra, she will be forsaken. For example, if a commanding general is fainthearted, his soldiers will become cowards. If a bow is weak, the bowstring will be slack. If the wind is gentle, the waves will never rise high. This all accords with the principles of nature. (WND, 464)

Faith in this sutra means that you will surely attain Buddhahood if you are true to the entirety of the Lotus Sutra, adhering exactly to its teachings without adding any of your own ideas or following the arbitrary interpretations of others. (WND, 1030)

Kyo'o's misfortune will change into fortune. Muster your faith, and pray to this Gohonzon. Then what is there that cannot be achieved? There can be no doubt about the sutra passages that say, "This sutra can fulfill their desires, as a clear cool pond can satisfy all those who are thirsty," and "They will enjoy peace and security in their present existence and good circumstances in future existences." (WND, 412)

People to Know

KYO'O

Nichiren once addressed a letter to Kyo'o, the infant daughter of Shijo Kingo and Nichigen-nyo, in response to news that she had fallen seriously ill. In this letter, Nichiren encourages her parents to muster the power of faith to cure their daughter's illness. "Nam-myoho-renge-kyo is like the roar of lion," he wrote them. "What sickness can therefore be an obstacle?"

Whether or not your prayer is answered will depend upon your faith; [if it is not] I will in no way be to blame. When the water is clear, the moon is reflected. When the wind blows, the trees shake. Our minds are like the water. Faith that is weak is like muddy water, while faith that is brave is like clear water. Understand that the trees are like principles, and the wind that shakes them is like the recitation of the sutra. (WND, 1079)

How, then, are you to go about nurturing faith in the Lotus Sutra? For if you try to practice the teachings of the sutra without faith, it would be like trying to enter a jeweled mountain without hands [to pick up its treasures], or like trying to make a thousand-mile journey without feet. The answer is simply to examine the proof that is close at hand, and thus to take hold of faith that is far off. (WND, 511)

What is called faith is nothing unusual. Faith means putting one's trust in the Lotus Sutra, Shakyamuni, Many Treasures, the Buddhas and bodhisattvas of the ten directions, and the heavenly gods and benevolent deities, and chanting Nam-myoho-renge-kyo as a woman cherishes her husband, as a man lays down his life for his wife, as parents refuse to abandon their children, or as a child refuses to leave its mother. (WND, 1036)

Strengthen your faith day by day and month after month. Should you slacken in your resolve even a bit, devils will take advantage. (WND, 997)

Faith in Daily Life

FAITH MANIFESTS IN DAILY LIFE

Faith in Buddhism is not an abstract concept separate from day-to-day reality. Our faith directly affects every aspect of our daily lives, from our beliefs about ourselves, our relationships with friends and family, to our contributions in society. Through faith, we gain the courage to take action and become experts at living. Those who show care and compassion to others, strive to excel at work and contribute to their communities show themselves to be people of genuine faith. Without such action, our faith becomes a mere formality.

Faith is the basic requirement for entering the way of the Buddha. In the fifty-two stages of bodhisattva practice, the first ten stages, dealing with faith, are basic, and the first of these ten stages is that of arousing pure faith. Though lacking in knowledge of Buddhism, a person of faith, even if dull-witted, is to be reckoned as a person of correct views. But even though one has some knowledge of Buddhism, if one is without faith, then one is to be considered a slanderer and an icchantika, or person of incorrigible disbelief. (WND, 141–42)

FAMILY RELATIONSHIPS

These are the two sufferings confronting you now. In order to expiate the sin of your past slanders, you are opposed by your parents, who hold mistaken views, and must live in the age of a ruler who persecutes the votary of the Lotus Sutra. The sutra makes this absolutely clear. Never doubt that you slandered the correct teaching in the past. If you have doubt about this, you will be unable to withstand the minor sufferings of this life. Then you may give in to your father's opposition and desert the Lotus Sutra against your will. (WND, 497)

Thus the blessings that you yourself enjoy are in fact treasures belonging to your late father. When the pine flourishes, the cypress will rejoice; when the grasses wither, the orchids weep. And if even feelingless beings such as plants and trees can behave in this way, then how much more so those who have feelings, let alone those who are bound together as father and son? (WND, 513)

In all worldly affairs, it is the son's duty to obey his parents, yet on the path to Buddhahood, disobeying one's parents ultimately constitutes filial piety. The Contemplation on the Mind-Ground Sutra explains the essence of filial piety: "By renouncing one's obligations and entering the Buddhist life one can truly repay those obligations in full." That is, in order to enter the true way, one leaves one's home against one's parents' wishes and attains Buddhahood. Then one can truly repay one's debt of gratitude to them. (WND, 499)

Priests possessed by the heavenly devil, such as Ryokan and the others, deceived your father, Saemon no Tayu, and tried to destroy you and your brother, but you, having a wise heart, heeded Nichiren's admonitions. Therefore, just as two wheels support a cart, or two legs carry a person, just as two wings enable a bird to fly, or just as the sun and moon aid all living beings, the efforts of you brothers have led your father to take faith in the Lotus Sutra. (WND, 845)

I do not know how to thank you for the sincerity you have shown in sending these articles. In the end, it must be an indication of the depth of the late Nanjo's faith in the Lotus Sutra. This is what is meant by the statement that a minister proclaims his ruler's sincerity, while a son proclaims his father's sincerity. The late Nanjo is probably delighted. (WND, 675)

Who but a son would have gone to such lengths to search for his father? The Venerable Maudgalyayana saved his mother from the sufferings of the world of hungry spirits, and the brothers Pure Storehouse and Pure Eye persuaded their father to give up his erroneous views. This is why it is said that a good child is a parent's treasure. (WND, 1045)

In the same document you say that you recall gratefully how, when your deceased father was still alive, you, my disciple, journeyed a thousand *ri* over mountains and rivers [to this distant place], receiving in person from me the daimoku of the Mystic Law, and how, less than thirty days later, your father's life came to an end. You say that although, alas, he has now become mere white bones in the dew garden of Jambudvipa, that although he has turned to dust and earth, you believe that his departed spirit will surely blossom into a flower of enlightenment in the land of Eagle Peak. (WND, 1061)

In the end it is nothing other than the loving kindness with which the woman cares for her child that makes the difference. Her concern concentrates on one thing just like the Buddhist practice of concentration. She thinks of nothing but her child, which is similar to Buddhist compassion. That must be why, although she created no other causes to bring it about, she was reborn in the Brahma heaven. (WND, 283)

Since I have realized that only the Lotus Sutra teaches the attainment of Buddhahood by women, and that only the Lotus is the sutra of true requital for repaying the kindness of our mother, in order to repay my debt to my mother, I have vowed to enable all women to chant the daimoku of this sutra. (WND, 931)

I hope that, if you, [Shichiro Goro's] loving mother, are thinking with longing about your son, you will chant Nam-myoho-renge-kyo and pray to be reborn in the same place as the late Shichiro Goro and your husband, the late Nanjo. The seeds of one kind of plant are all the same; they are different from the seeds of other plants. If all of you nurture the same seeds of Myoho-renge-kyo in your hearts, then you all will be reborn together in the same land of Myoho-renge-kyo. When the three of you are reunited there face to face, how great your joy will be! (WND, 1074)

Above all, both you and your husband are upholders of the Lotus Sutra. You will surely bear a jewel of a child who is going to inherit the seed for the propagation of the Lotus Sutra. I wholeheartedly congratulate you. The child is the one who will inherit both your physical and spiritual aspects. (WND, 186)

Kai-ko said: " . . . I felt it a terrible pity that someone such as he, outstanding in every respect, should die so young. Reconsidering the matter, however, I realized that it was because of this boy's death that his mother became a seeker of the way and his father began to practice, praying for his repose. How marvelous, I thought. Moreover, the fact that they have put their trust in the Lotus Sutra, which all people detest, must mean that their deceased son has been at their side and encouraged them to do so." I also believe this to be the case. (WND, 1050)

The Venerable Maudgalyayana put his faith in the Lotus Sutra, which is the greatest good there is, and thus not only did he himself attain Buddhahood, but his father and mother did so as well. And, amazing as it may seem, all the fathers and mothers of the preceding seven generations and the seven generations that followed, indeed, of countless lifetimes before and after, were able to become Buddhas. (WND, 820)

The debt of gratitude owed to one's father and mother is as vast as the ocean. If one cares for them while they are alive but does nothing to help them in their next life, it will be like a mere drop of water. (WND, 1033)

People to Know

NICHIREN'S PARENTS

Nichiren's parents were poor fisherfolk from southeastern Japan. After nearly escaping injury from a hostile crowd after he first proclaimed Nam-myoho-renge-kyo, he visited his parents and converted them to his teachings.

In any event, even though the parents may be evildoers, if the child is good, the parents' offenses will be forgiven. On the other hand, although the child may be an evildoer, if the parents are good persons, their child's faults will be pardoned. Hence, even though your late son, Yashiro, committed evil, if you, the mother who gave birth to him, grieve for him and offer prayers for him day and night in the presence of Shakyamuni Buddha, how could he not be saved? Moreover, because he believed in the Lotus Sutra, he may have become the one who will lead his parents to Buddhahood. (WND, 664)

FORTUNE

What good karma you must have formed in the past, then, to have been born a person able to recite even so much as a verse or a phrase of the Lotus Sutra! (WND, 69)

When one comes to the end of one's good fortune, no strategy whatsoever avails. When one's karmic rewards are exhausted, even one's retainers no longer follow one. You survived because you still have both good fortune and rewards. (WND, 1000)

Those who now believe in the Lotus Sutra will gather fortune from ten thousand miles away. (WND, 1137)

What fortune is mine to expiate in one lifetime the offenses of slandering the Law I have accumulated from the infinite past! How delighted I am to serve Shakyamuni Buddha, the lord of teachings, whom I have never seen! I pray that before anything else I can guide and lead the ruler and those others who persecuted me. I will tell the Buddha about all the disciples who have aided me, and before I die, I will transfer the great blessings deriving from my practice to my parents who gave me life. (WND, 402)

It is extremely rare to be born as a human being. Not only are you endowed with human form, but you have had the rare fortune to encounter Buddhism. Moreover, out of the Buddha's many teachings you have encountered the daimoku, or the title, of the Lotus Sutra and become its votary. Truly you are a person who has offered alms to a hundred thousand million Buddhas in his past existences! (WND, 993)

When one has had the rare good fortune to be born a human being, and the further good fortune to encounter the teachings of Buddhism, how can one waste this opportunity? If one is going to take faith at all, then among all the various teachings of the Mahayana and the Hinayana, provisional and true doctrines, one should believe in the one

People to Know

HOJO TOKIYORI

As regent of the Kamakura shogunate, Hojo Tokiyori grappled with threats of foreign invasion, natural disasters and internal conflict. Nichiren addressed his treatise "On Establishing the Correct Teaching for the Peace of the Land" to Tokiyori with the intention of sharing the value of the Lotus Sutra in changing such social and political strife.

vehicle, the true purpose for which the Buddhas come into the world and the direct path to attaining enlightenment for all living beings. (WND, 60)

Misfortune comes from one's mouth and ruins one, but fortune comes from one's heart and makes one worthy of respect. (WND, 1137)

Even though one neither reads nor studies the sutra, chanting the title alone is the source of tremendous good fortune. The sutra teaches that women, evil men, and those in the realms of animals and hell—in fact, all the beings of the Ten Worlds—can attain Buddhahood in their present form. [This is an incomparably greater wonder than] fire being produced by a stone taken from the bottom of a river, or a lantern lighting up a place that has been dark for a hundred, a thousand, or ten thousand years. If even the most ordinary things of this world are such wonders, then how much more wondrous is the power of the Buddhist Law! (WND, 923)

During [Sudatta's] last period of poverty, when all the people had fled or perished and only he and his wife remained, they had five measures of rice that would nourish them for five days. At that time, five people— Mahakashyapa, Shariputra, Ananda, Rahula and Shakyamuni Buddha—came one after another to beg for the five measures of rice, which Sudatta gave them. From that day on, Sudatta was the wealthiest man in all India, and he built the Jetavana Monastery. From this, you should understand all things. (WND, 1086)

FRIENDSHIP

When a tree has been transplanted, though fierce winds may blow, it will not topple if it has a firm stake to hold it up. But even a tree that has grown up in place may fall over if its roots are weak. Even a feeble person will not stumble if those supporting him are strong, but a person of considerable strength, when alone, may fall down on an uneven path. (WND, 598)

In this evil latter age, evil companions are more numerous than the dust particles that comprise the land, while good friends are fewer than the specks of dirt one can pile on a fingernail. (WND, 598)

Chang-an writes, "If one befriends another person but lacks the mercy to correct him, one is in fact his enemy." The consequences of a grave offense are extremely difficult to erase. The most important thing is to continually strengthen our wish to benefit others. (WND, 625)

Reflections

DIALOGUE

"In his landmark treatise 'On Establishing the Correct Teaching for the Peace of the Land,' which takes the form of a dialogue between a traveler and a host, the host (representing the Daishonin) never at any point raises his voice. On the contrary, when the guest becomes agitated, the host soothes him, smiles brightly and tenaciously continues the dialogue. We can take it that the Daishonin depicts the host in such a way because this was how he himself conducted dialogue."
—Daisaku Ikeda

The best way to attain Buddhahood is to encounter a good friend. How far can our own wisdom take us? If we have even enough wisdom to distinguish hot from cold, we should seek out a good friend. But encountering a good friend is the hardest possible thing to do. For this reason, the Buddha likened it to the rarity of a one-eyed turtle finding a floating log with a hollow in it the right size to hold him, or to the difficulty of trying to lower a thread from the Brahma heaven and pass it through the eye of a needle on the earth. (WND, 598)

If there is one who can cause others to awaken to and take faith in a teaching such as this, then that person is their father and mother, and also their good friend. This is a person of wisdom. (WND, 620–21)

FUNDAMENTAL DARKNESS

The great lantern that illuminates the long night of the sufferings of birth and death, the sharp sword that severs the fundamental darkness inherent in life, is none other than the Lotus Sutra. (WND, 1038)

The sutras preached prior to the Lotus Sutra seem to extinguish people's earthly desires [associated with their six sense organs], but in reality they do not. In contrast, the Lotus Sutra conquers the fundamental darkness [from which all earthly desires originate]. (WND, 646)

The great demon of fundamental darkness can even enter the bodies of bodhisattvas who have reached near-perfect enlightenment and prevent them from attaining the Lotus Sutra's blessing of perfect enlightenment. How easily can he then obstruct those in any lower stage of practice! (WND, 496)

GOHONZON

This mandala is in no way my invention. It is the object of devotion that depicts Shakyamuni Buddha, the World-Honored One, seated in the treasure tower of Many Treasures Buddha, and the Buddhas who were Shakyamuni's emanations as perfectly as a print matches its woodblock. Thus the five characters of the Lotus Sutra's title are suspended in the center, while the four heavenly kings are seated at the four corners of the treasure tower. (WND, 831)

I, Nichiren, have inscribed my life in sumi ink, so believe in the Gohonzon with your whole heart. The Buddha's will is the Lotus Sutra, but the soul of Nichiren is nothing other than Nam-myoho-renge-kyo. (WND, 412)

This Gohonzon also is found only in the two characters for faith. This is what the sutra means when it states that one can "gain entrance through faith alone." Since Nichiren's disciples and lay supporters believe solely in the Lotus Sutra, honestly discarding expedient means and not accepting even a single verse of the other sutras, exactly as the Lotus teaches, they can enter the treasure tower of the Gohonzon. How reassuring! (WND, 832)

I am entrusting you with a Gohonzon for the protection of your young child. This Gohonzon is the essence of the Lotus Sutra and the eye of all the scriptures. It is like the sun and the moon in the heavens, a great ruler on earth, the heart in a human being, the wish-granting jewel among treasures, and the pillar of a house. When we have this mandala with us, it is a rule that all the Buddhas and gods will gather round and watch over us, protecting us like a shadow day and night, just as warriors guard their ruler, as parents love their children, as fish rely on water, as trees and grasses crave rain, and as birds depend on trees. You must trust in it with all your heart. (WND, 624)

Faith in Daily Life

WHERE'S THE GOHONZON?

The scroll we refer to as the Gohonzon is a physical representation of our enlightened life-potential and not any external deity. As Nichiren taught, the real Gohonzon is within. He inscribed the scroll as the tool for us to reveal the indestructible happiness we already have within us. Though believers often praise the Gohonzon's power, the Gohonzon does not bestow benefit. Rather, benefits arise as a natural result of a believer's faith and practice.

Believe in the Gohonzon, the supreme object of devotion in all of Jambudvipa. Be sure to strengthen your faith, and receive the protection of Shakyamuni, Many Treasures, and the Buddhas of the ten directions. (WND, 386)

GONGYO

To accept, uphold, read, recite, take delight in, and protect all the eight volumes and twenty-eight chapters of the Lotus Sutra is called the comprehensive practice. To accept, uphold, and protect the "Expedient Means" chapter and the "Life Span" chapter is called the abbreviated practice. And simply to chant one four-phrase verse or the daimoku, and to protect those who do so, is called the essential practice. Hence, among these three kinds of practice, comprehensive, abbreviated, and essential, the daimoku is defined as the essential practice. (WND, 143)

The heart of the Lotus Sutra is its title, or the daimoku, of Nam-myoho-renge-kyo. Truly, if you chant this in the morning and evening, you are correctly reading the entire Lotus Sutra. Chanting daimoku twice is the same as reading the entire sutra twice, one hundred daimoku equal one hundred readings of the sutra, and one thousand daimoku, one thousand readings of the sutra. Thus, if you ceaselessly chant daimoku, you will be continually reading the Lotus Sutra. (WND, 923)

As I said before, though no chapter of the Lotus Sutra is negligible, among the entire twenty-eight chapters, the "Expedient Means" chapter and the "Life Span" chapter are particularly outstanding. The remaining chapters are all in a sense the branches and leaves of these two chapters. Therefore, for your regular recitation, I recommend that you practice reading the prose sections of the "Expedient Means" and "Life Span" chapters. (WND, 71)

First of all, when it comes to the Lotus Sutra, you should understand that, whether one recites all eight volumes, or only one volume, one chapter, one verse, one phrase, or simply the daimoku, or title, the blessings are the same. It is like the water of the great ocean, a single drop of which contains water from all the countless streams and rivers, or like the wish-granting jewel, which, though only a single jewel, can shower all kinds of treasures upon the wisher. (WND, 69)

I have written out the prose section of the "Expedient Means" chapter for you. You should recite it together with the verse portion of the "Life Span" chapter, which I sent you earlier. The characters of this sutra are all without exception living Buddhas of perfect enlightenment. But because we have the eyes of ordinary people, we see them as characters. (WND, 486)

GOOD AND EVIL

You have offered this sword to the Lotus Sutra. While you wore it at your side, it was an evil sword, but now that it has been offered to the Buddha, it has become a sword for good, just like a demon who conceives a desire to attain the Buddha way. How wondrous, how wondrous! (WND, 451)

While the rice itself is the same, rice that nourishes a slanderer of the Law supports the life of one who destroys the seeds of Buddhahood, enabling him to become a more powerful enemy than ever. And yet, does it not sustain his life so that he will in the end be won over to the Lotus Sutra? On the other hand, rice that nourishes the votary of the Lotus Sutra must be rice of the utmost compassion, because it benefits all living beings. (WND, 1117)

Opposing good is called evil, opposing evil is called good. Therefore, outside of the heart there is neither good nor evil. (GZ, 563)

To see evil and fail to admonish it, to be aware of slander and not combat it, is to go against the words of the sutras and to disobey the Buddhist patriarchs. (WND, 129)

The mystic principle of the true aspect of reality is one, but if it encounters evil influences, it will manifest delusion, while if it encounters good influences, it will manifest enlightenment. Enlightenment means

---

Faith in Daily Life

WHAT IS "EVIL" IN BUDDHISM?

Stemming from the fundamental darkness that is inherent in all life, evil is that which obstructs people in their Buddhist practice, robbing them of life force and causing them to doubt their own Buddhahood. Evil can be transformed into good to the extent that we use it as stimulus to deepen our faith and practice and strengthen our inherent goodness.

enlightenment to the essential nature of phenomena, and delusion, ignorance of it. It is like the case of a person who in a dream sees himself performing various good and evil actions. After he wakes up and considers the matter, he realizes that it was all a dream produced by his own mind. This mind of his corresponds to the single principle of the essential nature of phenomena, the true aspect of reality, while the good and evil that appeared in the dream correspond to enlightenment and delusion. When one becomes aware of this, it is clear that one should discard the ignorance associated with evil and delusion, and take as one's basis the awakening that is characterized by goodness and enlightenment. (WND, 417–18)

In the phrase "consistency from beginning to end," "beginning" indicates the root of evil and the root of good, and "end" indicates the outcome of evil and the outcome of good. One who is thoroughly awakened to the nature of good and evil from their roots to their branches and leaves is called a Buddha. (WND, 1121)

If people favor what is only incidental and forget what is primary, can the

---

People to Know

SAIREN-BO

Sairen-bo, a learned priest of another Buddhist school, observed how Nichiren, humbly clad in rags, would confidently debate and refute haughty priests dressed in fine robes. He converted to Nichiren's teachings after witnessing Nichiren's courage and comprehensive understanding of Buddhist scriptures.

---

benevolent deities be anything but angry? If people cast aside what is perfect and take up what is biased, can the world escape the plots of demons? Rather than offering up ten thousand prayers for remedy, it would be better simply to outlaw this one evil. (WND, 15)

I explained the teachings of the Lotus Sutra to you before. Matters of minor importance arise from good, but when it comes to a matter of great importance, great disaster without fail changes into great fortune. (WND, 824)

Just as poisonous compounds are changed into medicine, so these five characters of Myoho-renge-kyo change evil into good. (WND, 1064)

Though a person may do good, in the course of doing a single good deed he accumulates ten evil ones, so that in the end, for the sake of a small good, he commits great evil. And yet, in his heart, he prides himself on having practiced great good—such are the times we live in. (WND, 68–69)

Great events never have minor omens. When great evil occurs, great good follows. Since great slander already exists in our land, the great correct Law will spread without fail. What could any of you have to lament? Even if you are not the Venerable Mahakashyapa, you should all perform a dance. Even if you are not Shariputra, you should leap up and dance. When Bodhisattva Superior Practices emerged from the earth, did he not emerge dancing? (WND, 1119)

GREED

The point of this sutra is that the three poisons of greed, anger, and foolishness can become the seeds of Buddhahood. (WND, 228)

When their lives come to an end, within three days their bodies will turn into water that washes away, into dust that mixes with the earth, and into smoke that rises up into the sky, leaving no trace behind. Nevertheless, they seek to nurture these bodies and to amass great wealth. (WND, 891)

But if we examine the behavior of the priests of today who supposedly observe the precepts, we find that they hoard silks, wealth, and jewels, and concern themselves with lending money at interest. Since their doctrines and their practices differ so greatly, who would think of putting any faith in them? (WND, 102)

Never conduct yourself in a shameful manner. Be unmoved by greed, by the desire for fame, or by anger. (WND, 796)

Reflections

LIFETIME ENCOURAGEMENT

"We can sense the profound compassion of the Daishonin in each passage of his encouragement, which seems to say: 'I know you are suffering now, but I am your friend for life. I will send you encouragement and support as long as I live.'"
—Daisaku Ikeda

GRUDGES

If someone excels in this world, then even those who are regarded as worthies and sages, to say nothing of ordinary people, will all become jealous and bear grudges against that person. (WND, 940)

Though people may hate me, they cannot possibly alter the fact of my enlightenment. (WND, 384)

Worthy persons deserve to be called so because they are not carried away by the eight winds: prosperity, decline, disgrace, honor, praise, censure, suffering, and pleasure. They are neither elated by prosperity nor grieved by decline. The heavenly gods will surely protect one who is unbending before the eight winds. But if you nurse an unreasonable grudge against your lord, they will not protect you, not for all your prayers. (WND, 794)

And yet the Buddha harbored no grudges even against such enemies. How, then, could he ever cast aside anyone who had even once put faith in him? (WND, 510)

In the Lotus Sutra, it is stipulated that those who bear a grudge against its votary are destined to fall into the Avichi hell. The fourth volume states that the offense of harboring malice toward a votary of the Lotus Sutra in the latter age is graver than that of reviling the Buddha for an entire medium kalpa. (WND, 892)

I, Nichiren, am hated by the people of Japan. This is entirely due to the fact that the lord of Sagami regards me with animosity. I grant that the government has acted quite without reason, but even before I encountered my difficulties, I foresaw that troubles of this kind would occur, and I resolved that, whatever might happen to me in the future, I must not bear any hatred toward others. This determination has perhaps acted as a prayer, for I have been able to come safely through any number of trials. (WND, 686)

If the Law that one embraces is supreme, then the person who embraces it must accordingly be foremost among all others. And if that is so, then to speak ill of that person is to speak ill of the Law, just as to show contempt for the child is to show contempt for the parents. (WND, 61)

HAPPINESS

My disciples, you should believe what I say and watch what happens. These things do not occur because I myself am respectworthy, but because the power of the Lotus Sutra is supreme. If I praise myself, people will think that I am boastful, but if I humble myself, they will despise the sutra. The taller the pine tree, the longer the wisteria vine hanging from it. The deeper the source, the longer the stream. How fortunate, how joyful! In this impure land, I alone enjoy happiness and delight. (WND, 642)

I pray that you will embrace the Mystic Law, which guarantees that people "will enjoy peace and security in their present existence and good circumstances in future existences." This is the only glory that you need seek in your present lifetime, and is the action that will draw you toward Buddhahood in your next existence. Single-mindedly chant Nam-myoho-renge-kyo and urge others to do the same; that will remain as the only memory of your present life in this human world. (WND, 64)

Could "enjoy themselves at ease" mean anything but that both our bodies and minds, lives and environments, are entities of three thousand realms in a single moment of life and Buddhas of limitless joy?

People to Know

TOKI JONIN

Toki Jonin was one of Nichiren's most prominent disciples, whom he entrusted with many of his most important writings. He protected Nichiren from harm, and eagerly shared his letters with other lay followers. When Nichiren was exiled to Sado, Toki Jonin became a key disciple in encouraging Nichiren's followers in Kamakura to forge on.

There is no true happiness other than upholding faith in the Lotus Sutra. This is what is meant by "peace and security in their present existence and good circumstances in future existences." (WND, 681)

When the world makes you feel downcast, you should chant Nam-myoho-renge-kyo, remembering that, although the sufferings of this life are painful, those in the next life could be much worse. And when you are happy, you should remember that your happiness in this life is nothing but a dream within a dream, and that the only true happiness is that found in the pure land of Eagle Peak, and with that thought in mind, chant Nam-myoho-renge-kyo. (WND, 760)

There is no true happiness for human beings other than chanting Nam-myoho-renge-kyo. The sutra reads, " . . . where living beings enjoy themselves at ease." How could this passage mean anything but the boundless joy of the Law? (WND, 681)

HARDSHIPS

Though worldly troubles may arise, never let them disturb you. No one can avoid problems, not even sages or worthies. (WND, 681)

The greater the hardships befalling him, the greater the delight he feels, because of his strong faith. Doesn't a fire burn more briskly when logs are added? All rivers flow into the sea, but does the sea turn back their waters? The currents of hardship pour into the sea of the Lotus Sutra and rush against its votary. The river is not rejected by the ocean; nor does the votary reject suffering. Were it not for the flowing rivers, there would be no sea. Likewise, without tribulation there would be no votary of the Lotus Sutra. (WND, 33)

The heavenly devil hates the Buddha's Law, and the non-Buddhist believers resent the path of the Buddhist teachings. But you must be like the golden mountain that glitters more brightly when scraped by the wild boar, like the sea that encompasses all the various streams, like the fire that burns higher when logs are added, or like the kalakula insect that grows bigger when the wind blows. If you follow such examples, then how can the outcome fail to be good? (WND, 134)

If you truly fear the sufferings of birth and death and yearn for nirvana, if you carry out your faith and thirst for the way, then the sufferings of change and impermanence will become no more than yesterday's dream, and the awakening of enlightenment will become today's reality. (WND, 130)

The Nirvana Sutra teaches the principle of lessening one's karmic retribution. If one's heavy karma from the past is not expiated within this lifetime, one must undergo the sufferings of hell in the future, but if one experiences extreme hardship in this life [because of the Lotus Sutra], the sufferings of hell will vanish instantly. (WND, 199)

Setting aside for now the question of my wisdom, in enduring hardship and in suffering injury as an ally of the Lotus Sutra, I surpass even the Great Teacher T'ien-t'ai of China and excel even the Great Teacher Dengyo of Japan. This is because the time has made it so. (WND, 1070)

When I think that I will surely eradicate these karmic impediments and in the future go to the pure land of Eagle Peak, though various grave

---

Fast Facts

EXILE TO IZU

Nichiren never held back in his convictions. Thus he gained the scorn of many Nembutsu followers for his criticism of the erroneous views of the day. The Kamakura government banished Nichiren to Ito in Izu Province in 1261 after a failed attempt to assassinate him at Matsubagayatsu. When Nichiren was later abandoned en route, a fisherman named Funamori Yasaburo and his wife took him in. They later became his ardent followers.

persecutions fall on me like rain and boil up like clouds, since they are for the sake of the Lotus Sutra, even these sufferings do not seem like sufferings at all. (WND, 191)

From here we are going to cross the sea to the island province of Sado, but at the moment the winds are not favorable, so I do not know when we will depart. The hardships along the way were worse than I could have imagined, and indeed more than I can put down in writing. I will leave you to surmise what I endured. But I have been prepared for such difficulties from the outset, so there is no point in starting to complain about them now. I shall accordingly say no more of the matter. (WND, 206)

HEART

First of all, as to the question of where exactly hell and the Buddha exist, one sutra states that hell exists underground, and another sutra says that the Buddha is in the west. Closer examination, however, reveals that both exist in our five-foot body. This must be true because hell is in the heart of a person who inwardly despises his father and disregards his mother. It is like the lotus seed, which contains both blossom and fruit. In the same way, the Buddha dwells within our hearts. (WND, 1137)

You must pray to the heavenly gods with all your heart. Be ever diligent in your faith so that your desire will be fulfilled. (WND, 452)

More valuable than treasures in a storehouse are the treasures of the body, and the treasures of the heart are the most valuable of all. From the time you read this letter on, strive to accumulate the treasures of the heart! (WND, 851)

Flint has the potential to produce fire, and gems have intrinsic value. We ordinary people can see neither our own eyelashes, which are so close, nor the heavens in the distance. Likewise, we do not see that the Buddha exists in our own hearts. (WND, 1137)

Though the moon is forty thousand yojanas high in the heavens, its reflection appears instantly in a pond on earth; and the sound of the drum at the Gate of Thunder is immediately heard a thousand, ten thousand *ri* in the distance. Though you remain in Sado, your heart has come to this province. The way of attaining Buddhahood is just like this. Though we live in the impure land, our hearts reside in the pure land of Eagle Peak. Merely seeing each other's face would in itself be insignificant. It is the heart that is important. (WND, 949)

Fast Facts

WHERE IS THE BUDDHA LAND?

From the standpoint of Buddhism, the place where there are people awakened to their inherent potential becomes a place of infinite value, or a Buddha Land. The term also refers to the enlightened state or absolute happiness that one enjoys through faith.

It is the heart that is important. No matter how earnestly Nichiren prays for you, if you lack faith, it will be like trying to set fire to wet tinder. Spur yourself to muster the power of faith. Regard your survival as wondrous. Employ the strategy of the Lotus Sutra before any other. (WND, 1000-01)

The kalpa of decrease has its origin in the human heart. As the poisons of greed, anger, and foolishness gradually intensify, the life span of human beings gradually decreases and their stature diminishes. (WND, 1120)

HOPE

Those who believe in the Lotus Sutra are as if in winter, but winter always turns to spring. Never, from ancient times on, has anyone heard or seen of winter turning back to autumn. Nor have we ever heard of a believer in the Lotus Sutra who turned into an ordinary person. The sutra reads, "If there are those who hear the Law, then not a one will fail to attain Buddhahood." (WND, 536)

Money serves various purposes according to our needs. The same is true of the Lotus Sutra. It is a lantern in the dark or a boat at a crossing. At times it is water and, at times, fire. This being so, the Lotus Sutra assures us of "peace and security in our present existence and good circumstances in future existences." (WND, 452)

ILLNESS

In this age, it is as natural for a woman to change her fixed karma by practicing the Lotus Sutra as it is for rice to ripen in fall or chrysanthemums to bloom in winter. When I prayed for my mother, not only was her illness cured, but her life was prolonged by four years. Now you too have fallen ill, and as a woman, it is all the more timely for you to establish steadfast faith in the Lotus Sutra and to see what it will do for you. (WND, 955)

A person's death is not determined by illness. In our own time, the people of Iki and Tsushima, though not suffering from illness, were slaughtered in an instant by the Mongols. It is not certain that, because one is ill, one will die. And could not this illness of your husband's be the Buddha's design,

People to Know

MYOICHI

Myoichi was suffering from poor health when she wrote to Nichiren. A widow and a mother of two, she worried about dying and leaving her children alone to fend for themselves. Nichiren told her that "winter always turns to spring," and that with faith, any suffering can turn into benefit and joy. He urged her to never doubt the protection her faith would bring her.

because the Vimalakirti and Nirvana sutras both teach that sick people will surely attain Buddhahood? Illness gives rise to the resolve to attain the way. (WND, 937)

Is it true that there is illness in your family? If so, it cannot be the work of demons. Probably the ten demon daughters are testing the strength of your faith. No demon worthy of the name would even think of troubling a votary of the sutra and having its head broken. Persist in your faith with the firm conviction that both Shakyamuni Buddha and the Lotus Sutra are free from any falsehood. (WND, 899)

Many people, both high and low, have admonished or threatened you, but you have refused to give up your faith. Since you now appear certain to attain Buddhahood, perhaps the heavenly devil and evil spirits are using illness to try to intimidate you. Life in this world is limited. Never be even the least bit afraid! (WND, 1109)

Life is the most precious of all treasures. Even one extra day of life is worth more than ten million *ryo* of gold. The Lotus Sutra surpasses all the other sacred teachings of the Buddha's lifetime because of the "Life Span" chapter. The greatest prince in the land of Jambudvipa would be of less consequence than a blade of grass if he died in childhood. If he died young, even a person whose wisdom shone as brilliantly as the sun would be less than a living dog. So you must hasten to accumulate the treasure of faith and quickly conquer your illness. (WND, 955)

I have heard that you are suffering from illness. Is this true? The impermanence of this world is such that even the healthy cannot remain forever, let alone those who are ill. Thoughtful persons should therefore prepare their minds for the life to come. Yet one cannot prepare one's mind for the next life by one's own efforts alone. Only on the basis of the teachings of Shakyamuni Buddha, the original teacher of all living beings, can one do so. (WND, 76)

The lion king is said to advance three steps, then gather himself to spring, unleashing the same power whether he traps a tiny ant or attacks a fierce animal. In inscribing this Gohonzon for [your daughter's] protection, Nichiren was like the lion king. This is what the sutra means by "the power [of the Buddhas] that has the lion's ferocity." Believe in this mandala with all your heart. Nam-myoho-renge-kyo is like the roar of a lion. What sickness can therefore be an obstacle? (WND, 412)

You also are a practitioner of the Lotus Sutra, and your faith is like the waxing moon or the rising tide. Be deeply convinced, then, that your illness cannot possibly persist, and

Reflections

BUDDHISM IS PRACTICAL

"To think of Buddhism as a placid teaching expounded in a bucolic setting under the shade of a tree is a totally false image. Buddhism is intensely practical, not escapist. It lives in human society and has been handed down among the people—this is the true flow of Buddhism." —Daisaku Ikeda

Receiving a letter from their beloved mentor gave many
followers new hope to overcome various problems.

that your life cannot fail to be extended! Take care of yourself, and do not burden your mind with grief. (WND, 656)

If you are unwilling to make efforts to heal yourself, it will be very difficult to cure your illness. One day of life is more valuable than all the treasures of the major world system, so first you must muster sincere faith. (WND, 955)

My greatest concern now is your illness. Fully convinced that you will recover your health, you should continue moxibustion treatment for three years, as regularly as if you had just begun. Even those who are free from illness cannot escape the transience of life, but you are not yet old, and because you are a votary of the Lotus Sutra, you will not meet an untimely death. Your illness is surely not due to karma, but even if it were, you could rely on the power of the Lotus Sutra to cure it. (WND, 656)

INCORRECT TEACHINGS

For those who have faith in the Lotus Sutra, but whose faith is not deep, it is as though a half moon were lighting the darkness. But for those who have profound faith, it is as though a full moon were illuminating the night. (WND, 94)

When one must face enemies, one needs a sword, a stick, or a bow and arrows. When one has no enemies, however, such weapons are of no use at all. In this age, the provisional teachings have turned into enemies of the true teaching. When the time is right to propagate the teaching of the one vehicle, the provisional teachings become enemies. When they are a source of confusion, they must be thoroughly refuted from the standpoint of the true teaching. Of the two types of practice, this is shakubuku, the practice of the Lotus Sutra. (WND, 394)

When one falls into such an evil place, the fact that one was a ruler or a general means nothing. Tormented by the wardens of hell, one is no different than a monkey on a string. What use are fame and fortune then? Can one still be arrogant and persist in false beliefs? (WND, 1026)

To mix other practices with this Nam-myoho-renge-kyo is a grave error. A lantern is useless when the sun rises. How can dewdrops be beneficial when the rain falls? Should one feed a newborn baby anything other

---

Faith in Daily Life

NO PLACE FOR AUTHORITARIANS

History is filled with examples of religious figures demanding unquestioning obedience. Nichiren abhorred such authoritarianism and rebuked priests of other schools who were obsessed with fame and fortune. He criticized them for forgetting their purpose to care for people. Moreover, he urged people to not be blinded by someone's status, always maintaining a critical eye and using the scriptures as their spiritual compass.

than its mother's milk? No addition of other medicines is needed with a good medicine. (WND, 903)

It is a rare thing to be born as a human being. And if, having been born as such, you do not do your best to distinguish between the correct doctrine and the incorrect so that in the future you may attain Buddhahood, then you are certainly not fulfilling your true worth as a human being. (WND, 350)

A sutra says: "Rely on the Law and not upon persons. Rely on the meaning of the teaching and not on the words. Rely on wisdom and not on discriminative thinking. Rely on sutras that are complete and final and not on those that are not complete and final." The meaning of this passage is that one should not rely upon the words of the bodhisattvas and teachers, but should heed what was established by the Buddha. (WND, 872–73)

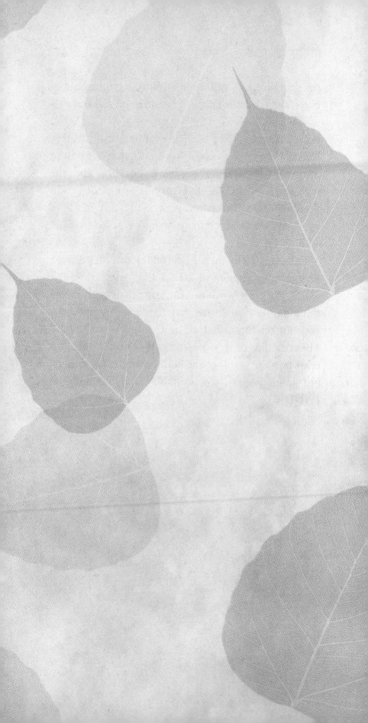

JOY

My actions seem to be in exact accord with what the sutra teaches. Therefore, whenever I meet great difficulties, I am more delighted than if my deceased parents had returned to life, or than one who sees the person one hates meet with some mishap. I am overjoyed that I, a foolish man, should be regarded as a sage by the Buddha. (WND, 799)

There is no doubt . . . that in my present life I am the votary of the Lotus Sutra, and that in the future I will therefore reach the seat of enlightenment without fail. Judging the past from this point of view, I must have been at the Ceremony in the Air. There can be no discontinuity between the three existences of past, present, and future. Because I view things this way, I feel immeasurable delight even though I am now an exile. Joy as well as sorrow moves us to tears. Tears express our feelings for both blessings and misfortune. (WND, 386)

I am but an ignorant ordinary person made of flesh and blood; I have not rid myself of even a fraction of the three categories of illusion. Yet, on account of the Lotus Sutra, I have been reviled, slandered, attacked with swords and staves, and sent into exile. In light of these persecutions, I believe I may be likened to the great sages who burned their arms, crushed their marrow, or did not begrudge being beheaded. This is what I mean by immense joy. (WND, 45)

When you chant the daimoku of this sutra, you should be aware that it is a more joyful thing than for one who was born blind to gain sight and see one's father and mother, and a rarer thing than for a man who has been seized by a powerful enemy to be released and reunited with his wife and children. (WND, 143)

I cannot hold back my tears when I think of the great persecution confronting me now, or when I think of the joy of attaining Buddhahood in the future. (WND, 386)

From a mundane view, I am the poorest person in Japan, but in the light of Buddhism, I am the wealthiest person in all Jambudvipa. When I consider that this is all because the time is right, I am overwhelmed with joy and cannot restrain my tears. (WND, 977)

I think I have practiced the Lotus Sutra twenty-four hours each day and night. I say so because, having been exiled on the Lotus Sutra's account, I now read and practice it continuously, whether I am walking, standing, sitting, or lying down. For anyone born human, what greater joy could there be? (WND, 43)

K

KARMA

My followers are now able to accept and uphold the Lotus Sutra because of the strong ties they formed with it in their past existences. They are certain to obtain the fruit of Buddhahood in the future. The heritage of the Lotus Sutra flows within the lives of those who never forsake it in any lifetime whatsoever—whether in the past, the present, or the future. (WND, 217)

People say that, if you tie a piece of living rhinoceros horn to your body and enter the water, the water will not come within five feet of you. They also say that, if one leaf of the sandalwood tree unfurls, it can eradicate the foul odor of the eranda trees for a distance of forty yojanas. In this case, our evil karma may be likened to the eranda trees or the

Faith in Daily Life

LESSENING KARMIC RETRIBUTION

Everyone must experience the effects of their bad karma from the past, but Buddhist faith allows us to experience it to a lesser degree. This is particularly the case when we experience hardship because we practice Buddhism, as happened to Nichiren. He courageously underwent persecution and taught his followers that experiencing such hardships on account of their faith is the surest way to change their destiny.

water, and the daimoku of the Lotus Sutra may be likened to the rhinoceros horn or the sandalwood leaf. (WND, 142)

It is like the example of the Ganges River. Hungry spirits see the waters of the river as fire, human beings see them as water, and heavenly beings see them as amrita. The waters are the same in all cases, but each type of being sees them differently, according to the effects of its karma. (WND, 517)

It is impossible to fathom one's karma. Iron, when heated in the flames and pounded, becomes a fine sword. Worthies and sages are tested by abuse. My present exile is not because of any secular crime. It is solely so that I may expiate in this lifetime my past grave offenses and be freed in the next from the three evil paths. (WND, 303)

There are two types of illness: minor and serious. Early treatment by a skilled physician can cure even serious illnesses, not to mention minor ones. Karma also may be divided into two categories: fixed and unfixed. Sincere repentance will eradicate even fixed karma, to say nothing of karma that is unfixed. (WND, 954)

Reflections

STEADY GROWTH

"The heritage of the ultimate law of life exists only within our own lives. The spirit of this Gosho lives only within a life that continues to grow from day to day and month to month."   —Daisaku Ikeda

Our worldly misdeeds and evil karma may have piled up as high as Mount Sumeru, but when we take faith in this sutra, they will vanish like frost or dew under the sun of the Lotus Sutra. (WND, 1026)

When iron is heated, if it is not strenuously forged, the impurities in it will not become apparent. Only when it is subjected to the tempering process again and again will the flaws appear. When pressing hemp seeds, if one does not press very hard, one will not get much oil from them. Likewise, when I vigorously berate those throughout the country who slander the Law, I meet with great difficulties. It must be that my actions in defending the Law in this present life are calling forth retributions for the grave offenses of my past. (WND, 281-82)

Usually these sufferings appear one at a time, on into the boundless future, but Nichiren has denounced the enemies of the Lotus Sutra so severely that all eight have descended at once. This is like the case of a peasant heavily in debt to the steward of his village and to other authorities. As long as he remains in his village or district, rather than mercilessly hounding him, they are likely to defer his debts from one year to the next. But when he tries to leave, they rush over and demand that he repay everything at once. (WND, 305)

Amber draws dust, and a magnet attracts iron particles; here our evil karma is like the dust or iron, and the daimoku of the Lotus Sutra is like the amber or the magnet. If we consider these [analogies, we can see why] we should always chant Nam-myoho-renge-kyo. (WND, 142)

KNOWLEDGE AND FAITH

"Knowledge without faith" describes those who are knowledgeable about the Buddhist doctrines but have no faith. These people will never attain Buddhahood. Those of "faith without knowledge" may lack knowledge but have faith and can attain Buddhahood. This is not merely my own opinion; it is stated clearly in the Lotus Sutra. (WND, 1030)

It is the way of scholars these days to assert that only those who possess superior wisdom and strenuously exert themselves in the practice of meditation have the capacity to benefit from the Lotus Sutra, and to discourage persons who lack wisdom from even trying. But this is in fact an utterly ignorant and erroneous view. The Lotus Sutra is the teaching that enables all living beings to attain the

Fast Facts

FOR THE COMMON PERSON

Nichiren composed his letters to believers in the common phonetic script instead of classical Chinese characters. After his death, the five senior priests other than Nikko were ashamed of his language style, seen to be less scholarly, and destroyed many letters. Fortunately, more than four hundred writings have survived until today.

Buddha way. Therefore, the persons of superior faculties and superior capacity should naturally devote themselves to contemplation and to meditating on the Law. But, for persons of inferior faculties and inferior capacity, the important thing is simply to have a heart of faith. (WND, 59)

Even a wise person cannot become a Buddha through the other sutras, but with the Lotus Sutra, even fools can plant the seeds that lead to Buddhahood. As the sutra passage I have quoted earlier puts it, "Although they do not seek emancipation, emancipation will come of itself." (WND, 283)

Question: Is it possible, without understanding the meaning of the Lotus Sutra, but merely by chanting the five or seven characters of Nam-myoho-renge-kyo once a day, once a month, or simply once a year, once a decade, or once in a lifetime, to avoid being drawn into trivial or serious acts of evil, to escape falling into the four evil paths, and instead to eventually reach the stage of non-regression?
Answer: Yes, it is. (WND, 141)

If a physician gives medicine to a sick person, even though the sick person may not know the origin and nature of the medicine, if he takes it, then in the natural course of events his illness will be cured. But if he objects that he does not know the origin of the medicine that the physician gives him and for that reason declines to take it, do you think his illness will ever be cured? Whether he understands the medicine or not, so long as he takes it, he will in either case be cured. (WND, 132)

Chudapanthaka was unable to memorize a teaching of fourteen characters even in the space of three years, and yet he attained Buddhahood. Devadatta, on the other hand, had committed to memory sixty thousand teachings but fell into the hell of incessant suffering. These examples exactly represent the situation in the world in this present latter age. Never suppose that they pertain only to other people and not to yourselves. (WND, 602)

LEADERSHIP

If a boat is handled by an unskilled steersman, it may capsize and drown everyone aboard. Likewise, though someone may have great physical strength, if he lacks a resolute spirit, even his many abilities will be of no use. (WND, 614)

In battles soldiers regard the general as their soul. If the general were to lose heart, his soldiers would become cowards. (WND, 613)

When praised highly by others, one feels that there is no hardship one cannot bear. Such is the courage that springs from words of praise. (WND, 385)

LIFE

Rice may seem like a very small thing, yet it is what sustains human life. And the Buddha says that life is something that cannot be purchased even for the price of an entire major world system. (WND, 983)

The most dreadful things in the world are the pain of fire, the flashing of swords, and the shadow of death. Even horses and cattle fear being killed; no wonder human beings are afraid of death. Even a leper clings

Bringing happiness to people's daily lives was
Nichiren's greatest wish.

to life; how much more so a healthy person. The Buddha teaches that even filling the entire major world system with the seven kinds of treasures does not match offering one's little finger to the Buddha and the [Lotus] sutra. (WND, 301)

Life is the foremost of all treasures. It is expounded that even the treasures of the entire major world system cannot equal the value of one's body and life. Even the treasures that fill the major world system are no substitute for life. (WND, 1125)

Life at each moment encompasses the body and mind and the self and environment of all sentient beings in the Ten Worlds as well as all insentient beings in the three thousand realms, including plants, sky, earth, and even the minutest particles of dust. Life at each moment permeates the entire realm of phenomena and is revealed in all phenomena. To be awakened to this principle is itself the mutually inclusive relationship of life at each moment and all phenomena. (WND, 3)

A single life is worth more than the major world system. You still have many years ahead of you, and moreover you have encountered the Lotus Sutra. If you live even one day longer, you can accumulate that much more benefit. How truly precious your life is! (WND, 955)

How swiftly the days pass! It makes us realize how few are the years we have left. Friends enjoy the cherry blossoms together on spring mornings, and then they are gone, carried away like the blossoms by the winds of impermanence, leaving nothing but their names. Although the blossoms have scattered, the cherry trees will bloom again with the coming of spring, but when will those people be reborn? (WND, 1027)

LOSS OF A LOVED ONE

Though I have long since ceased to think about my home, seeing this laver brings back many familiar memories, and I am saddened and find it hard to bear. It is the same kind of laver I saw long ago on the shore at Kataumi, Ichikawa, and Kominato. I feel an unwarranted resentment that, while the color, shape, and taste of this laver have remained unchanged, my parents have passed away, and I cannot restrain my tears. (WND, 466)

In your letter you mentioned your filial devotion to your deceased mother. Reading it, I was so moved that I could barely hold back my tears. (WND, 442)

Perhaps your deceased son has become a Buddha and, in order to guide his father and mother, has entered your hearts. The king Wonderful Adornment was an evil king. However, because his two sons, Pure Storehouse and Pure Eye, guided him to the way, he and his wife were both able to place their trust in the Lotus Sutra and become Buddhas. Mysteriously enough, your own circumstances are much the same. (WND, 1050)

But the sorrow of having lost one's parent or child seems only to deepen as the days and months pass. Yet although death is sorrowful in any case, for parents to die and their children to live on is the natural course of things. It is pitiful indeed for an aged mother to be preceded by her child in death! You may well feel resentment toward both the gods and Buddhas. Why did they not take you instead of your son? Why did they let you survive only to be tormented by such grief? It must be truly hard to bear. (WND, 662)

The boy Snow Mountains was able to give his body for half a verse of a Buddhist teaching, and Bodhisattva Medicine King was able to burn his arms as an offering to the Buddha because both were sages, and it was like pouring water on fire. But your husband was an ordinary person, so it was like putting paper in fire. Therefore, he must certainly have received blessings as great as theirs. He is probably watching his wife and children in the heavenly mirrors of the sun and moon every moment of the day and night. Since you and your children are ordinary persons, you cannot see or hear him; neither can the deaf hear thunder nor the blind see the sun. But never doubt that he is protecting you. (WND, 536)

Because your beloved departed father chanted Nam-myoho-renge-kyo while he was alive, he was a person who attained Buddhahood in his present form, in the same way that stones change into jewels. (WND, 1064)

In the same way that, when King Rinda hears the sound of the horses, his complexion brightens and his strength increases, when your beloved deceased father hears the sound of your voice chanting Nam-myoho-renge-kyo, he will delight in his Buddhahood. (WND, 1066)

In your letters in the past, you have from time to time mentioned your concern for your parents. And when I read your present letter, I could not hold back my tears, so moved was I by pity at your sorrow over the thought that your parents might perhaps be in hell. . . . But now you have already manifested a sincere concern for your parents, and the heavenly gods are certain to heed your prayers. (WND, 686)

You must have been firmly convinced that when you died you would be carried by him on his back to the graveyard, and that there would be nothing left for you to worry about. But lamentably, he has preceded you in death. "Why? Why did this happen? It must be a dream, an illusion! I will wake up; I will wake up!" you must have thought. But without your having awakened, already one year has given way to the next. You do not know how long you will have to wait. . . . And yet there is a way to meet him readily. With Shakyamuni Buddha as your guide, you can go to meet him in the pure land of Eagle Peak. (WND, 1091–92)

It is certain that, even if there were an age when the sun rises in the west, or a time were to come when the moon emerges from the ground, the Buddha's words would never prove false. Judging from this, there cannot be the least doubt that your late father is now in the presence of Shakyamuni Buddha, the lord of teachings, and that you will receive great blessings in your present existence. How wonderful, how splendid! (WND, 655)

LOTUS SUTRA

Birds and crickets cry, but never shed tears. I, Nichiren, do not cry, but my tears flow ceaselessly. I shed my tears not for worldly affairs but solely for the sake of the Lotus Sutra. So, indeed, they must be tears of amrita. (WND, 386)

The Buddha is of course respectworthy, but when compared with the Lotus Sutra he is like a firefly beside the sun or moon. The superiority of the Lotus Sutra to Shakyamuni Buddha is as great as the distance from heaven to earth. Presenting offerings to the Buddha produces benefits like that. How much more so is this true of the Lotus Sutra? (WND, 899)

Thus a single word of this Lotus Sutra is as precious as a wish-granting jewel, and a single phrase is the seed of all Buddhas. (WND, 539)

The Buddha's utterances have become the works that compose the entire body of sutras and bring benefit to all living beings. And among the sutras, the Lotus Sutra is a manifestation in writing of the Thus Come One Shakyamuni's intent; it is his voice set down in written words. Thus the Buddha's heart is embodied in these written words. To illustrate, it is like seeds that sprout, grow into plants, and produce rice. Though the form of the rice changes, its essence remains the same. (WND, 333)

Moreover, as life does not go beyond the moment, the Buddha expounded the blessings that come from a single moment of rejoicing [on hearing the Lotus Sutra]. If two or three moments were required, this could no longer be called the original vow of the Buddha endowed with great impartial wisdom, the single vehicle of the teaching that directly reveals the truth and leads all living beings to attain Buddhahood. (WND, 62)

Metal has the power to cut down trees and plants, and water has the power to extinguish any kind of fire. In like manner, the Lotus Sutra has the power to bring all living beings to the state of Buddhahood. (WND, 512)

For more than forty years after the Thus Come One went out into the world, he did not reveal the true teaching. In the Lotus Sutra, he for the first time revealed the true way that leads to the attainment of Buddhahood. (WND, 57)

The men of Japan are like Devadatta, and the women are like the dragon king's daughter. Whether by following it or opposing it, they will attain Buddhahood through the Lotus Sutra. This is the message of the "Devadatta" chapter. (WND, 963–64)

No matter how firmly the sutras preached before the Lotus Sutra guarantee the attainment of Buddhahood, and no matter how much the believers in these provisional doctrines may wildly insist that this is so, it is as easy to refute these assertions as it is to smash a thousand earthen cooking dishes with a single hammer. This is what is meant by the statement "The Lotus Sutra is the teaching of shakubuku, the refutation of the provisional doctrines." The Lotus Sutra is indeed the most profound teaching. (WND, 963)

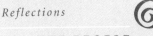

Reflections

FOR THE PEOPLE

"He did not seek personal status or honor. The Daishonin put his life on the line to speak out on behalf of society, the Law and the people."
—Daisaku Ikeda

If we are to believe these dying words of the Buddha, we must conclude that the Lotus Sutra is the only bright mirror we should have, and that through it we can understand the heart of all the sutras. (WND, 692)

The Lotus Sutra is none other than the scripture that reveals that Shakyamuni became a Buddha numberless major world system dust particle kalpas ago. It also predicts that Shariputra and the other disciples will become Buddhas in the future. (WND, 652)

The Lotus Sutra is the king of sutras, true and correct in both word and principle. Its words are the ultimate reality, and this reality is the Mystic Law (*myoho*). It is called the Mystic Law because it reveals the principle of the mutually inclusive relationship of a single moment of life and all phenomena. That is why this sutra is the wisdom of all Buddhas. (WND, 3)

Gold can be neither burned by fire nor corroded or swept away by water, but iron is vulnerable to both. A worthy person is like gold, a fool like iron. You are like pure gold because you embrace the "gold" of the Lotus Sutra. The sutra states, "Just as among all the mountains, Mount Sumeru is foremost, so this Lotus Sutra is likewise." It also states, "The good fortune you gain thereby . . . cannot be burned by fire or washed away by water." (WND, 217)

Fast Facts

ALL ABOUT TIMING

The Latter Day of the Law began two thousand years after Shakyamuni's death. It is characterized as a time when his teachings would become lost and fail to lead people directly to enlightenment. Nichiren stated that this is a time when the supreme teaching of the Lotus Sutra would be widely propagated.

Though I may be a person of little ability, I have reverently given myself to the study of the Mahayana. A blue fly, if it clings to the tail of a thoroughbred horse, can travel ten thousand miles, and the green ivy that twines around the tall pine can grow to a thousand feet. (WND, 17)

All the sacred teachings of Shakyamuni's lifetime are the golden words of the Thus Come One; for countless kalpas, they have never contained the slightest falsehood. The Lotus Sutra is the truth of all truths taught by the Buddha, for it includes his declaration of "honestly discarding expedient means." (WND, 954)

A wisteria vine, by twining around a pine, may climb a thousand fathoms into the air; and a crane, because it has its wings to rely upon, can travel ten thousand *ri*. It is not their own strength that allows them to do these things. This applies likewise in the case of the priest Jibu-bo. Though he himself is like the wisteria vine, because he clings to the pine that is the Lotus Sutra, he is able to ascend the mountain of perfect enlightenment. (WND, 820–21)

MARRIAGE/
PARTNERSHIP

The men with whom you have exchanged marriage vows over the course of all your previous lifetimes must outnumber even the grains of sand in the ocean. Your vows this time, however, were ones made with your true husband. The reason is that it was due to his encouragement that you became a practitioner of the Lotus Sutra. Thus you should revere him as a Buddha. (WND, 456)

Insects eat the trees they live in, and fish drink the water in which they swim. If grasses wither, orchids grieve; if pine trees flourish, cypresses rejoice. Even trees and plants are so closely related. The hiyoku is a bird with one body and two heads. Both of its mouths nourish the same body. Himoku are fish with only one eye each, so the male and female remain together for life. A husband and wife should be like them. (WND, 501-02)

Explain all this to your wife too, and work together like the sun and moon, a pair of eyes, or the two wings of a bird. With the sun and moon, could there be a path of darkness? With a pair of eyes, no doubt you will see the faces of Shakyamuni, Many Treasures, and the Buddhas of the ten directions. With a pair of wings, you will surely fly in an instant to the treasure land of Tranquil Light. (WND, 319)

A man is like a pillar, a woman like the crossbeam. A man is like the legs of a person, a woman like the trunk. A man is like the wings of a bird, a woman like the body. If the wings and the body become separated, then how can the bird fly? And if the pillar topples, then the crossbeam will surely fall to the ground. (WND, 1043)

You are like the two wings of a bird, or the two eyes of a person. And your wives are your support. Women support others and thereby cause others to support them. When a husband is happy, his wife will be fulfilled. If a husband is a thief, his wife will become one, too. This is not a matter of this life alone. A husband and wife are as close as a form and shadow, flowers and fruit, or roots and leaves, in every existence of life. (WND, 501)

A wife who leads her husband to take faith will enjoy the same benefit as Lady Pure Virtue. All the more fortunate is a case like yours, in which both wife and husband have faith! It is like a bird possessing two wings, or a cart having two wheels. What is there that you two cannot achieve? Because there is a heaven and an earth, a sun and a moon, the sun shines and the rain falls, and the plants and trees of benefit will surely blossom and bear fruit. (WND, 915)

MENTOR AND DISCIPLE

When all others hate me, the fact that you have placed even a bit of trust in me and, moreover, have come all the way here to visit me, cannot be ascribed to the karma of your present life alone. Surely we must share some bond from a previous existence! (WND, 610)

You accompanied Nichiren, vowing to give your life as a votary of the Lotus Sutra. Your deed is a hundred, thousand, ten thousand times greater than that of Hung Yen, who cut open his stomach and inserted the liver of his dead lord, Duke Yi [to save him from shame and dishonor]. When I reach Eagle Peak, I will first tell how Shijo Kingo, like myself, resolved to die for the Lotus Sutra. (WND, 196)

People to Know

SHIJO KINGO

Shijo Kingo, a samurai warrior by trade, became one of Nichiren's most devoted supporters. Despite criticism and persecution over his devotion to Nichiren, he remained steadfast. He even accompanied Nichiren to the execution grounds where he was to be beheaded, prepared to die at his mentor's side.

If there is someone who knows which of the Buddhist teachings are true and which are false, then I must seek him out, make him my teacher, and treat him with appropriate respect. (WND, 105)

Those who become Nichiren's disciples and lay believers should realize the profound karmic relationship they share with him and spread the Lotus Sutra as he does. Being known as a votary of the Lotus Sutra is a bitter, yet unavoidable, destiny. (WND, 994)

Nichiren alone took the lead in carrying out the task of the Bodhisattvas of the Earth. He may even be one of them. If Nichiren is to be counted among the Bodhisattvas of the Earth, then so must his disciples and lay supporters. (WND, 385)

A cub sired by a lion king will become a lion king; it will never become a human king or heavenly king. Now the votaries of the Lotus Sutra are the children of Shakyamuni Buddha, the lord of teachings, as the sutra states, "The living beings in it are all my children." It is not difficult for them to become kings of the Law just as Shakyamuni Buddha did. (WND, 323)

In view of our promise from the beginningless past and the principle that one will be constantly reborn with one's teacher, if I, Nichiren,

People to Know

NIKKO

Nikko proved himself to be Nichiren's most trusted disciple among the six senior priests. From a very young age, he devotedly served Nichiren, even accompanying him to exile on Sado Island and Izu. After Nichiren's death, he devoted himself to propagating Nichiren's teachings, educating disciples and collecting and transcribing Nichiren's writings.

attain Buddhahood in my present lifetime, then how could it be possible for you to become separated from me and fall into the evil paths? (WND, 312)

No one but Nichiren has ever revealed teachings like these. Though T'ien-t'ai, Miao-lo, and Dengyo knew about them in their hearts, they never put them into words. They went about their lives keeping this knowledge to themselves. And there was good reason for this. The Buddha had not entrusted them with the task, the time had not yet come, and they had not been the Buddha's disciples from the distant past. (WND, 383)

If a tree is deeply rooted, its branches and leaves will never wither. If the spring is inexhaustible, the stream will never run dry. Without wood, a fire will burn out. Without earth, plants will not grow. I, Nichiren, am indebted solely to my late teacher, Dozen-bo, for my having become the votary of the Lotus Sutra and my being widely talked about now, in both a good and bad sense. Nichiren is like the plant, and my teacher, the earth. (WND, 909)

In kindling a fire, three things are needed: a good piece of steel, a good flint, and good tinder. The same is true of prayer. Three things are required—a good teacher, a good believer, and a good teaching—before prayers can be effective and disasters banished from the land. (WND, 880)

You and I have been born together in this defiled age of the Latter Day of the Law, in the country of Japan in the southern continent of Jambudvipa, and with the utmost reverence we chant with our mouths Nam-myoho-renge-kyo, the ultimate reason for which the Buddhas appear in the world; we believe in it in our hearts, embrace it with our bodies, and delight in it with our hands. Has all of this not come about solely because of some bond of karma we share from the past? (WND, 309)

Even if a person of wisdom who embraces the correct teaching existed, how could he propagate it without lay believers who supported him? (WND, 752)

In any event, there can be no doubt about your enlightenment in your next life. Above all, I remember how, in the eighth year of the Bun'ei era (1271), when I incurred the wrath of the authorities and was about to be beheaded at Tatsunokuchi in the province of Sagami, you held on to the reins of my horse, accompanying me barefoot and shedding tears of grief. You were even prepared to give your life had I in fact been executed. In what lifetime could I possibly forget it? (WND, 1069)

I entreat the people of this country: Do not look down upon my disciples! If you inquire into their past, you will find that they are great bodhisattvas who have given alms to Buddhas over a period of eight hundred thousand million kalpas, and who have carried out practices under Buddhas as numerous as the sands of the Hiranyavati and Ganges rivers. And if we speak of the future, they will be endowed with the benefit of the fiftieth person, sur-passing that of one who gave alms to innumerable living beings for a period of eighty years. They are like an infant emperor wrapped in swaddling clothes, or a great dragon who has just been born. Do not despise them! Do not look on them with con-tempt! (WND, 788–89)

The rice plant flowers and bears grain, but its spirit remains in the soil. This is the reason the stalk sprouts to flower and bear grain once again. The blessings that Nichiren obtains from propagating the Lotus Sutra will always return to Dozen-bo. How sublime! It is said that, if a teacher has a good disciple, both will gain the fruit of Buddhahood, but if a teacher fosters a bad disciple, both will fall into hell. If teacher and disciple are of different minds, they will never accomplish anything. (WND, 909)

It must be ties of karma from the distant past that have destined you to become my disciple at a time like this. Shakyamuni and Many Treasures certainly realized this truth. The sutra's statement, "Those per-sons who had heard the Law dwelled here and there in various Buddha lands, constantly reborn in com-pany with their teachers," cannot be false in any way. (WND, 217)

While I was there, however, you and your husband, the lay priest of Ko, being apprehensive of the eyes of others, brought me food in the middle of the night. Never fearing even punishment from the provincial

Nichiren's devoted disciple, Shijo Kingo,
solemnly accompanied him to the execution
grounds at Tatsunokuchi.

officials, you are persons who were ready to sacrifice yourselves for me. Thus, though it was a harsh land, when I left, I felt as if the hair that had been shaved from my head were being tugged from behind and as if with each step I took I were being pulled back. (WND, 596)

Over and over I recall the moment, unforgettable even now, when I was about to be beheaded and you accompanied me, holding the reins of my horse and weeping tears of grief. Nor could I ever forget it in any lifetime to come. If you should fall into hell for some grave offense, no matter how Shakyamuni Buddha might urge me to become a Buddha, I would refuse; I would rather go to hell with you. For if you and I should fall into hell together, we would find Shakyamuni Buddha and the Lotus Sutra there. (WND, 850)

The Great Teacher Dengyo says: "Neither teacher nor disciples need undergo countless kalpas of austere practice in order to attain Buddhahood. Through the power of the Lotus Sutra of the Wonderful Law they can do so in their present form." This means that both the teacher who expounds the principles of the Lotus Sutra and the disciple who receives his teachings will, in no long time, together become Buddhas through the power of the Lotus Sutra. (WND, 133)

MIND OF FAITH

Those who practice with distorted views, however, are destroying this most precious sutra. You should simply be careful that, without differing thoughts, you single-mindedly aspire to the pure land of Eagle Peak. A passage in the Six Paramitas Sutra says to become the master of your mind rather than let your mind master you. (WND, 486)

The physical and spiritual, which are one in essence, manifest themselves as two distinct aspects; thus the Buddha's mind found expression as the written words of the Lotus Sutra. These written words are the Buddha's mind in a different form. Therefore, those who read the Lotus Sutra must not regard it as consisting of mere written words, for those words are in themselves the Buddha's mind. (WND, 86)

The Buddha wrote that one should become the master of one's mind rather than let one's mind master oneself. This is what I mean when I emphatically urge you to give up even your body, and never begrudge even your life for the sake of the Lotus Sutra. (WND, 390)

In propagating these five characters, practitioners should "not hesitate even if it costs them their lives." "Single-mindedly desiring to see the Buddha" may be read as follows: single-mindedly observing the Buddha, concentrating one's mind on seeing the Buddha, and when looking at one's own mind, perceiving that it is the Buddha. (WND, 389–90)

I chant the daimoku, which is the heart and core of the entire sutra, and I urge others to do likewise. Although the mugwort growing in a hemp field or wood marked for cutting with an inked line may not be straight to begin with, they will as a matter of course become so. In the same way, one who chants the daimoku as the Lotus Sutra teaches will never have a twisted mind. For one should know that, unless the mind of the Buddha enters into our bodies, we cannot in fact chant the daimoku. (WND, 670)

All the other sutras are examples of preaching in accordance with the minds of others, because, when expounding them, the Buddha adjusted himself to the minds of all other living beings. But the Lotus Sutra is an example of preaching in accordance with the Buddha's own mind, because in it the Buddha had all living beings comply with his own mind. (WND, 969)

A mind now clouded by the illusions of the innate darkness of life is like a tarnished mirror, but when polished, it is sure to become like a clear mirror, reflecting the essential nature of phenomena and the true aspect of reality. Arouse deep faith, and diligently polish your mirror day and night. How should you polish it? Only by chanting Nam-myoho-renge-kyo. (WND, 4)

If a vessel is free of these four faults of overturning, leaking, being defiled, and being mixed, then it can be called a perfect vessel. If the embankments around a moat do not leak, then the water will never escape from the moat. And if the mind of faith is perfect, then the water of wisdom, the great impartial wisdom, will never dry up. (WND, 1015)

MISGUIDED TEACHERS

When I observe carefully the state of the world today, I see people who give way to doubt because of the lack of understanding [on the part of eminent priests]. They look up at the heavens and mouth their resentment, or gaze down at the earth and sink deep into despair. (WND, 7)

One should abandon even one's teacher if he or she is misguided, though there will be cases where this is not necessary. One should decide according to the principles both of the world and of Buddhism. Priests in the Latter Day of the Law are ignorant of the principles of Buddhism and are conceited, so they despise the correct teacher and fawn on patrons. True priests are those who are honest and who desire little and yet know satisfaction. (WND, 747)

It is the nature of beasts to threaten the weak and fear the

Reflections

WRITINGS AS A GUIDE

"When the Daishonin is no longer in the world, it is his writings that we should make our mentor. So long as we continue practicing in accordance with the Gosho, what possible cause for confusion can there be?"   —Daisaku Ikeda strong. Our contemporary scholars of the various schools are just like them. They despise a wise man without power, but fear evil rulers. (WND, 302)

The Buddha stated that, in the latter age, monks and nuns with the hearts of dogs would be as numerous as the sands of the Ganges. By this he meant that the priests and nuns of that day would be attached to fame and fortune. Because they wear robes and surplices, they look like ordinary priests and nuns. But in their hearts they wield a sword of distorted views. (WND, 755)

Although people study Buddhism, it is difficult for them to practice it correctly either because of the ignorance of their minds, or because, even though wise, they fail to realize that they are being misled by their teachers. (WND, 894)

The Parinirvana Sutra states: "Those who enter the monastic order, don clerical garments, and make a show of studying my teachings will exist in ages to come. Being lazy and remiss, they will slander the correct and equal sutras. You should be aware that all these people are followers of the non-Buddhist doctrines of today." Those who read this passage should reflect deeply on their own practice. The Buddha is saying that those of our contemporary priests who wear clerical garments, but are idle and negligent, were disciples of the six non-Buddhist teachers in his day. (WND, 303)

People all turn their backs on these sutra passages, and the world as a whole is completely confused with regard to the principles of Buddhism. Why do you persist in following the teachings of evil friends? T'ien-t'ai said that to accept and put faith in the doctrines of evil teachers is the same as drinking poison. You should deeply consider this and beware! (WND, 61)

I had not felt that I should speak in this way; but I, too, cannot be exempted from the Buddha's warning that, if one sees a misguided priest sending others into hell with his evil teachings and fails to reproach that priest and expose his errors, then one is oneself betraying the Buddha's teaching. (WND, 807)

There are two kinds of wisdom, correct and perverse. No matter how wise a person may appear, if his assertions are warped you should not listen to him. Nor should you follow priests merely because they are venerable or of high rank. (WND, 1028)

These passages from the sutras speak of powerful enemies of the correct teaching. Such enemies are to be found not so much among evil rulers and evil ministers, among non-Buddhists and devil kings, or among monks who disobey the precepts. Rather they are those great slanderers of the Law who are to be found among the eminent monks who appear to be upholders of the precepts and men of wisdom. (WND, 584)

Because they appear to be true priests, the people trust them without the slightest doubt about what they preach. Therefore, without realizing it, the people who follow them have become enemies of the Lotus Sutra and foes of Shakyamuni Buddha. (WND, 923)

People to Know

HEI NO SAEMON

Hei no Saemon joined forces with the authorities of the day, such as the priest Ryokan, to ruin Nichiren's reputation. His harsh persecutions allowed Nichiren to encounter and overcome severe trials, thus helping him reveal his true mission as a great Buddhist sage.

NAM-MYOHO-RENGE-KYO

Those who chant Myoho-renge-kyo [the title of the Lotus Sutra] even without understanding its meaning realize not only the heart of the Lotus Sutra, but also the "main cord," or essential principle of the Buddha's lifetime teachings. (WND, 860)

Though the scaffolding is necessary to complete the pagoda, no one would ever dream of discarding the pagoda and worshiping the scaffolding. And yet the people who seek the way in the world today spend their whole lives reciting Namu Amida Butsu only, and never once chant Nam-myoho-renge-kyo. They are like persons who discard the pagoda and worship the scaffolding. (WND, 1074)

Those who uphold this sutra should be prepared to meet difficulties. It is certain, however, that they will "quickly attain the unsurpassed Buddha way." To "continue" means to cherish Nam-myoho-renge-kyo, the most important principle for all the Buddhas of the three existences. (WND, 471)

One who listens to even a sentence or phrase of the sutra and cherishes it deep in one's heart may be likened to a ship that crosses the sea of the sufferings of birth and death. The Great Teacher Miao-lo stated,

"Even a single phrase cherished deep in one's heart will without fail help one reach the opposite shore. To ponder one phrase and practice it is to exercise navigation." Only the ship of Myoho-renge-kyo enables one to cross the sea of the sufferings of birth and death. (WND, 33)

Our contemporaries think of the five characters of Myoho-renge-kyo only as a name, but this is not correct. It is the essence, that is, the heart of the Lotus Sutra. . . . Those who seek the heart of the sutra apart from its title are as foolish as the turtle who sought the monkey's liver outside the monkey, or the monkey who left the forest and sought fruit on the seashore. (WND, 861)

The Lotus Sutra of the Correct Law says that, if one hears this sutra and proclaims and embraces its title, one will enjoy merit beyond measure. And the Supplemented Lotus Sutra of the Wonderful Law says that one who accepts and upholds the name of the Lotus Sutra will enjoy immeasurable good fortune. These statements indicate that the good fortune one receives from simply chanting the daimoku is beyond measure. (WND, 143)

Therefore, when you chant *myoho* and recite *renge*, you must summon up deep faith that Myoho-renge-kyo is your life itself. (WND, 3)

Nam-myoho-renge-kyo is not only the core of the Buddha's lifetime teachings, but also the heart, essence, and ultimate principle of the Lotus Sutra. (WND, 860)

If you wish to free yourself from the sufferings of birth and death you have endured since time without beginning and to attain without fail unsurpassed enlightenment in this lifetime, you must perceive the mystic truth that is originally inherent in all living beings. This truth is Myoho-renge-kyo. Chanting Myoho-renge-kyo will therefore enable you to grasp the mystic truth innate in all life. (WND, 3)

Question: If a person simply chants Nam-myoho-renge-kyo with no understanding of its meaning, are the benefits of understanding thereby included?

Answer: When a baby drinks milk, it has no understanding of its taste, and yet its body is naturally nourished. Who ever took the wonderful medicines of Jivaka knowing of what they were compounded? Water has no intent, and yet it can put out fire. Fire consumes things, and yet how can we say that it does so consciously? (WND, 788)

Ignorant people should by all means have faith in the Lotus Sutra. For although one may think that all the titles of the sutras are the same in effect and that it is

---

Fast Facts

PROCLAMATION

Nichiren Daishonin was thirty-two when he concluded that Nam-myoho-renge-kyo was the essence of the Lotus Sutra and Shakyamuni's ultimate teaching for the enlightenment of all humanity.

---

as easy to chant one as another, in fact the merit acquired even by an ignorant person who chants the title of the Lotus Sutra is as far superior to that acquired by a wise person who chants some other title as heaven is to earth! (WND, 730–31)

Now, at the beginning of the Latter Day of the Law, I, Nichiren, am the first to embark on propagating, throughout Jambudvipa, the five characters of Myoho-renge-kyo, which are the heart of the Lotus Sutra and the eye of all Buddhas. (WND, 764–65)

Reflections

UNCHANGING TRUTHS

"The Gosho were written by Nichiren Daishonin with thirteenth century Japanese society as their setting. However, everywhere within and between the lines is the immutable truth of Buddhism, shining like a glistening jewel."

—Daisaku Ikeda

When once we chant Myoho-renge-kyo, with just that single sound we summon forth and manifest the Buddha nature of all Buddhas; all existences; all bodhisattvas; all voice-hearers; all the deities such as Brahma, Shakra, and King Yama; the sun and moon, and the myriad stars; the heavenly gods and earthly deities, on down to hell-dwellers, hungry spirits, animals, asuras, human and heavenly beings, and all other living beings. This blessing is immeasurable and boundless. (WND, 887)

A bird's egg contains nothing but liquid, yet by itself this develops into a beak, two eyes, and all the other parts, and the bird soars into the sky. We, too, are the eggs of ignorance, which are pitiful things, but when nurtured by the chanting of Nam-myoho-renge-kyo, which is like the warmth of the mother bird, we develop the beak of the thirty-two features and the feathers of the eighty characteristics and are free to soar into the sky of the true aspect of all phenomena and the reality of all things. (WND, 1030)

If only you chant Nam-myoho-renge-kyo, then what offense could fail to be eradicated? What blessing could fail to come? This is the truth, and it is of great profundity. You should believe and accept it. (WND, 130)

As we have seen, even those who lack understanding, so long as they chant Nam-myoho-renge-kyo, can avoid the evil paths. This is like lotus flowers, which turn as the sun does, though the lotus has no mind to direct it, or like the plantain that grows with the rumbling of thunder, though this plant has no ears to hear it. Now we are like the lotus or the plantain, and the daimoku of the Lotus Sutra is like the sun or the thunder. (WND, 142)

NEGATIVE INFLUENCES

No matter whom you may marry, if he is an enemy of the Lotus Sutra, you must not follow him. Strengthen your resolve more than ever. Ice is made of water, but it is colder than water. Blue dye comes from indigo, but when something is repeatedly dyed in it, the color is better than that of the indigo plant. The Lotus Sutra remains the same, but if you repeatedly strengthen your resolve, your color will be better than that of others, and you will receive more blessings than they do. (WND, 615)

You should take every care to ward off slanderers of the Law in the same way that you would never wish a courtesan even to come near your home. This is the meaning of "Thrust aside evil friends and associate with good companions." (WND, 832)

What one should fear is slander of the profound teaching as well as companions who are slanderers, for these will surely cause one to fall into the frightful Avichi hell. (WND, 620)

Reflections

GETTING GROUNDED IN STUDY

"The Daishonin's words are guiding principles that have universal, eternal relevance. It is important to study his writings. And it is especially crucial that the members of the youth division gain a grounding in Buddhist study."

—Daisaku Ikeda

Neither non-Buddhists nor the enemies of Buddhism can destroy the correct teaching of the Thus Come One, but the Buddha's disciples definitely can. As a sutra says, only worms born of the lion's body feed on the lion. (WND, 302)

The Great Teacher T'ien-t'ai commented, "If they encounter an evil friend, they will lose their true mind." "True mind" means the mind that believes in the Lotus Sutra, while "lose" means to betray one's faith in the Lotus Sutra and transfer one's allegiance to other sutras. The sutra reads, " . . . but when they are given the medicine, they refuse to take it." T'ien-t'ai stated, "Those who have lost their minds refuse to take the good medicine, even though it is given to them. Lost in the sufferings of birth and death, they run away to another land." (WND, 495)

No matter how honest and upright you may be, or how you may strive to be known as a worthy person in the secular or the religious world, if you associate with evil persons, then as a natural result you will find that in two or three instances out of ten you are following their teachings, and in the end you, too, will become an evil person. (WND, 310)

Although we may have a certain amount of faith, we may encounter evil influences and find our faith weakening. Then we will deliberately abandon our faith, or, even though we maintain our faith for a day, we will set it aside for a month. In such cases, we are like vessels that let the water leak out. (WND, 1014)

A person of great fortune will never be ruined by enemies, but may be ruined by those who are close. (WND, 302)

Only by defeating a powerful enemy can one prove one's real strength. (WND, 302)

Those who believe in the Lotus Sutra should beware of and guard themselves against the sutra's enemies. . . . . If you do not know your enemies, you will be deceived by them. (WND, 664)

NICHIREN

Names are important for all things. That is why the Great Teacher T'ient'ai placed "name" first among the five major principles. My giving myself the name Nichiren (Sun Lotus) derives from my own enlightenment regarding the Buddha vehicle. (WND, 993)

Nichiren is the son of a chandala family who lived near the sea in Tojo in Awa Province, in the remote countryside of the eastern part of Japan. How could giving up a body that will decay uselessly for the sake of the Lotus Sutra not be exchanging rocks for gold? None of you should lament for me. (WND, 202)

Fast Facts

SUN LOTUS

The name *Nichiren*, a name that he gave himself, actually contains two Chinese characters that mean "Sun" and "Lotus." Taking on the name Nichiren reveals his conviction that he will shed light upon the impure Latter Day of the Law and cause the blossoms of happiness to unfold amid the torment of society.

In this life, however, as the votary of the Lotus Sutra, I was exiled and put to death—exiled to Ito and beheaded at Tatsunokuchi. Tatsunokuchi in Sagami Province is the place where Nichiren gave his life. Because he died there for the Lotus Sutra, how could it be anything less than the Buddha land? (WND, 196)

I, Nichiren, am sovereign, teacher, and father and mother to all the people of Japan. (WND, 287)

All happened just as the Buddha had predicted, and there is no doubt that I, Nichiren, am the votary of the Lotus Sutra. (WND, 607)

The persecutions Nichiren has faced are the result of karma formed in previous lifetimes. The "Never Disparaging" chapter reads, "when his offenses had been wiped out," indicating that Bodhisattva Never Disparaging was vilified and beaten by countless slanderers of the correct teaching because of his past karma. How much more true this is of Nichiren, who in this life was born poor and lowly to a chandala family. . . . It is impossible to fathom one's karma. (WND, 303)

In the yard around the hut the snow piled deeper and deeper. No one came to see me; my only visitor was the piercing wind. *Great Concentration and Insight* and the Lotus Sutra lay open before my eyes, and Nam-myoho-renge-kyo flowed from my lips. My evenings passed in discourse to the moon and stars on the fallacies of the various schools and the profound

From a dilapidated hut on Sado Island, Nichiren
wrote some of his most important letters.

meaning of the Lotus Sutra. Thus, one year gave way to the next. (WND, 770–71)

After everyone had gone, I began to put into shape a work in two volumes called *The Opening of the Eyes*, which I had been working on since the eleventh month of the previous year. I wanted to record the wonder of Nichiren, in case I should be beheaded. The essential message in this work is that the destiny of Japan depends solely upon Nichiren. A house without pillars collapses, and a person without a soul is dead. Nichiren is the soul of the people of this country. (WND, 772)

On the twelfth day of the ninth month of last year, between the hours of the rat and the ox (11:00 P.M. to 3:00 A.M.), this person named Nichiren was beheaded. It is his soul that has come to this island of Sado and, in the second month of the following year, snow-bound, is writing this to send to his close disciples. (WND, 269)

Fast Facts

SADO ISLAND

After barely avoiding execution at Tatsunokuchi, Nichiren was banished to Sado Island in 1271, a place from which few thought he would ever return. There he was forced to inhabit a dilapidated hut in a graveyard, exposed to harsh weather. He suffered from a lack of food and water, but loyal followers helped him by making the perilous journey to bring provisions. During this time, Nichiren wrote many of his most important writings.

Donning the armor of endurance and girding myself with the sword of the wonderful teaching, I have raised the banner of the five characters of Myoho-renge-kyo, the heart of the entire eight volumes of the Lotus Sutra. Then, drawing the bow of the Buddha's declaration, "I have not yet revealed the truth," and notching the arrow of "honestly discarding the provisional teachings," I have mounted the carriage drawn by the great white ox and battered down the gates of the provisional teachings. (WND, 392)

The Lotus Sutra is the staff that helps all the Buddhas of the three existences as they set their minds on enlightenment. However, you should rely on Nichiren as your staff and pillar. When one uses a staff, one will not fall on treacherous mountain paths or rough roads, and when led by the hand, one will never stumble. (WND, 451)

The "Emerging from the Earth" chapter also explains something about me, because it states that Bodhisattva Superior Practices and his followers will appear in the Latter Day of the Law to propagate the five characters of Nam-myoho-renge-kyo. I, Nichiren, have appeared earlier than anyone else. How reassuring to think that I will no doubt be praised by bodhisattvas equal in number to the sands of sixty thousand Ganges Rivers! (WND, 964)

How wondrous it is that, around two hundred years and more into the Latter Day of the Law, I was the first to reveal as the banner of propagation of the

Lotus Sutra this great mandala that even those such as Nagarjuna and Vasubandhu, T'ien-t'ai and Miao-lo were unable to express. (WND, 831)

It may seem like self-praise on my part, but having pondered this, I will give credence to the words of the Buddha. I, the priest Nichiren, am the votary referred to in the scripture. (WND, 407)

I, Nichiren, have personally suffered each of the nine great ordeals. . . . These are hardships that T'ien-t'ai and Dengyo never met. Truly you should know that, adding Nichiren to the other three, there is now a fourth votary of the Lotus Sutra who has appeared in the Latter Day of the Law. How glad I am to fulfill the words of the prophecy from the sutra: "How much more will this be so after his passing?" (WND, 448)

Just as the Buddha's words in the sutra predict, the ruler grew hostile and the common people began

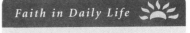

Faith in Daily Life

HUMAN REVOLUTION

Nichiren never used the modern term *human revolution*, but this term captures the essence of his teaching that we can develop our innate potential through faith. We cannot always see the potential we have within, so Nichiren used many analogies to illustrate this point. Whether through the lotus blooming in the muddy swamp, the promise of cherry blossoms in the spring, or the fluid inside an egg eventually becoming a bird, Nichiren urged his followers to revolutionize their lives.

Reflections

A KEEN DESIRE

"Some Gosho, of course, are very doctrinal and complex. But we do not necessarily have to understand all of the Daishonin's writings. The important thing is to have a keen desire to read the Gosho and to expose our lives, even for just a short time each day, to Nichiren Daishonin's spirit."
—Daisaku Ikeda

to attack me. And because they treated me with enmity, heaven grew enraged, the sun and moon displayed great changes in their behavior, and huge comets appeared. The earth shook as though it would turn over, internecine strife broke out, and they were attacked by a foreign country. All happened just as the Buddha had predicted, and there is no doubt that I, Nichiren, am the votary of the Lotus Sutra. (WND, 607)

OBSTACLES

Whatever obstacles I might encounter, so long as persons of wisdom do not prove my teachings to be false, I will never yield! All other troubles are no more to me than dust before the wind. (WND, 280)

[T'ien-t'ai writes:] "As practice progresses and understanding grows, the three obstacles and four devils emerge in confusing form, vying with one another to interfere. . . One should be neither influenced nor frightened by them. If one falls under their influence, one will be led into the paths of evil. If one is frightened by them, one will be prevented from practicing the correct teaching." This statement not only applies to me, but also is a guide for my followers. Reverently make this teaching your own, and transmit it as an axiom of faith for future generations. (WND, 501)

Even though one may encounter a wise teacher and the true sutra and thereby embrace the correct teaching, when one resolves to break free from the sufferings of birth and death and attain Buddhahood, one will inevitably encounter seven grave matters known as the three obstacles and four devils, just as surely as a shadow follows the body and clouds accompany rain. Even if you should manage to overcome the first six, if you are defeated by the seventh, you will not be able to become a Buddha. (WND, 894)

There is definitely something extraordinary in the ebb and flow of the tide, the rising and setting of the moon, and the way in which summer, autumn, winter, and spring give way to each other. Something uncommon also occurs when an ordinary person attains Buddhahood. At such a time, the three obstacles and four devils will invariably appear, and the wise will rejoice while the foolish will retreat. (WND, 637)

The wonderful means of truly putting an end to the physical and spiritual obstacles of all living beings is none other than Nam-myoho-renge-kyo. (WND, 842)

OFFERINGS

In your position as a woman, you have made offerings to the Lotus Sutra in this defiled latter age. Therefore, the heavenly king Brahma will look after you with his divine eye, Shakra will press his palms together and pay obeisance to you, the earthly deities will delight in reverently holding up your feet, and Shakyamuni Buddha will extend his hand from Eagle Peak to pat your head. (WND, 981)

This passage means that the blessings from making offerings to a votary of the Lotus Sutra in the evil age of the Latter Day of the Law surpass those from earnestly making offerings with one's words, thoughts, and deeds for the space of an entire medium kalpa to a Buddha such as Shakyamuni. Though this seems impossible, you must never doubt it, because these are the Buddha's golden words. (WND, 595)

Shakyamuni Buddha teaches, however, that one who makes offerings to the votary of the Lotus Sutra in the latter age for even a single day will gain benefit a hundred, thousand, ten thousand, million times greater than one would by offering countless treasures to the Buddha for one million kalpas. (WND, 1097)

Those who offer even a flower or a stick of incense to such a sutra have offered alms to a hundred thousand million Buddhas in their previous existences. (WND, 654)

In the past, the boy Virtue Victorious offered a mud pie to the Buddha, and was reborn as King Ashoka ... A poor woman cut off her hair and sold it to buy oil [for the Buddha], and not even the winds sweeping down from Mount Sumeru could extinguish the flame of the lamp fed by this oil. Accordingly, your offerings of two and three strings of coins are far greater even than those of the ruler of Japan, who may offer the nation and build a pagoda adorned with the seven kinds of treasures that reaches to the heaven of the thirty-three gods. (WND, 1089)

Though often in dire poverty themselves,
Nichiren's disciples sent provisions—such as rice,
paper, coins or cloth—to ease his harsh living
conditions while in exile.

Those who give alms and support to the votary will receive the same benefit as though making offerings to the Lotus Sutra itself. (WND, 1133)

Though one may perform meritorious deeds, if they are directed toward what is untrue, then those deeds may bring great evil, but they will never result in good. On the other hand, though one may be ignorant and make meager offerings, if one presents those offerings to a person who upholds the truth, one's merit will be great. How much more so in the case of people who in all sincerity make offerings to the correct teaching! (WND, 1134)

Even if one does no harm to others and honestly strives to make offerings, there will be cases in which one does not attain Buddhahood. To illustrate, if one plants good seed in a bad field, the seed itself will be ruined, and one will in turn suffer loss. Even if one is sincere, if the person to whom one makes offerings is evil, those offerings will fail to produce benefit; rather, they will cause one to fall into the evil paths. (WND, 1103)

ORDINARY PEOPLE

The heart of the Lotus Sutra is the revelation that one may attain supreme enlightenment in one's present form without altering one's status as an ordinary person. This means that without casting aside one's karmic impediments one can still attain the Buddha way. Thus T'ien-t'ai said, "The other sutras only predict Buddhahood . . . for the good, but not for the evil; . . . This [Lotus] sutra predicts Buddhahood for all." (WND, 410)

Because of the difference between ordinary people and Buddhas that stems from the disparity between delusion and enlightenment, ordinary people are unaware that they are endowed with both the entity and the functions of the three bodies. (WND, 384)

I, Nichiren, have been able to endure countless harsh trials. When praised, one does not consider one's personal risk, and when criticized, one can recklessly cause one's own ruin. Such is the way of common mortals. (WND, 385)

Though it is thought that Shakyamuni Buddha possesses the three virtues of sovereign, teacher, and parent for the sake of all of us living beings, that is not so. On the contrary, it is common mortals who endow him with the three virtues. (WND, 384)

[The Nirvana Sutra] compares "it gradually becomes deeper" to the Lotus Sutra leading everyone, from ordinary people who lack understanding to sages who possess it, to attain the Buddha way. (WND, 39)

Though water may be pure at the outset, if it becomes muddied, the moon does not shine in it. But even though night soil is filthy, when it clears, the moon does not begrudge its reflection. The muddied water may be pure in nature, yet the moon does not shine in it. But the night soil, though impure in nature,

reflects the moon's rays when it clears. The muddy water may be likened to learned priests and eminent scholars who keep the precepts but turn their backs on the Lotus Sutra. The night soil may be likened to ignorant people without precepts whose greed is profound and whose anger is intense, but who put undivided faith in the Lotus Sutra alone.
(WND, 1082)

But if a person has the wisdom to know the true meaning of the Lotus Sutra, no matter how lowly he may appear, pay respect to him and make offerings to him as though he were a living Thus Come One. Thus it is written in the sutra. That is why the Great Teacher Dengyo says that the men and women who believe in this sutra, even if they lack knowledge or violate the precepts, should be seated above priests who observe all two hundred and fifty precepts of the Hinayana teachings, and never be seated in a humble position, and that this is all the more true of the priests of this Mahayana sutra. (WND, 1028)

Faith in Daily Life

HERITAGE OF FAITH

The spirit with which Nichiren practiced Buddhism is the model for all his followers. He set the example for a life of happiness and victory. To make the Daishonin's spirit our own is what we refer to as the heritage, or lifebloood, of faith. Rather than through formal ceremonies or secret teachings, we inherit this lifeblood through our own efforts to practice as Nichiren did, thus reaping the ultimate rewards of Buddhist practice.

Never seek this Gohonzon outside yourself. The Gohonzon exists only within the mortal flesh of us ordinary people who embrace the Lotus Sutra and chant Nam-myoho-renge-kyo. (WND, 832)

An ordinary person is a Buddha, and a Buddha, an ordinary person. This is what is meant by three thousand realms in a single moment of life and by the phrase "I in fact attained Buddhahood." (WND, 36)

PEACE

The Buddha, sensing his sincerity, emerged from beneath the earth and taught him as follows:

"Practice what accords with the Law; do not practice what contradicts it. One who practices the Law will dwell in peace and security both in this life and in the next." (WND, 321)

If the nation is destroyed and people's homes are wiped out, then where can one flee for safety? If you care anything about your personal security, you should first of all pray for order and tranquillity throughout the four quarters of the land, should you not? (WND, 24)

Fast Facts

FINAL WILL

Before Nichiren died, he gave lectures about "On Establishing the Correct Teaching for the Peace of the Land," one of the first treatises he ever wrote. Submitted to the Kamakura government, it discussed the causes of some of the major social problems of the day, including the threat of foreign invasion, drought and internal strife. He pointed out the misconceptions of other Buddhist schools and urged the authorities to adopt the principles of the Lotus Sutra as a response to these great social problems. Nichiren's lifetime teachings began and ended with this seminal treatise for the sake of peace.

When the world is at peace, worthies are hard to distinguish. It is when the age is in turmoil that both sages and fools come into view. (WND, 845)

Countless people study the non-Buddhist works known as the *Three Records* and the *Five Canons*, but not even one case in ten million is found where a person governs society and behaves as the texts teach. Thus it is very difficult to establish peace in society. One may be letter-perfect in reciting the Lotus Sutra, but it is far more difficult to act as it teaches. (WND, 200)

PERSECUTION

I spoke out solely because I had long known that the people of Japan would meet with great suffering, and I felt pity for them. Thoughtful persons should therefore realize that I have met these trials for their sake. If they were people who understood their obligations or were capable of reason, then out of two blows that fall on me, they would receive one in my stead. (WND, 828)

A fire burns higher when logs are added, and a strong wind makes a kalakula grow larger. The pine tree lives for ten thousand years, and therefore its boughs become bent and twisted. The votary of the Lotus Sutra is like the fire and the kalakula, while his persecutions are like the logs and the wind. (WND, 471)

Although I, Nichiren, am not a man of wisdom, the devil king of the sixth heaven has attempted to take possession of my body. But I have for some time been taking such great care that he now no longer comes near me. Therefore, because the power of the heavenly devil is ineffectual against me, he instead possesses the ruler and his high officials, or foolish priests such as Ryokan, and causes them to hate me. (WND, 310)

I was nearly beheaded at Tatsunokuchi, wounded on the forehead [at Komatsubara], and slandered time and again. My disciples have also been exiled and thrown into prison, and my lay supporters have been evicted and had their fiefs confiscated. How can the persecutions faced by Nagarjuna, T'ien-t'ai, or Dengyo possibly compare with these? (WND, 395)

Considering how disasters have struck one after another in the wake of my exile, would they dare attempt to harass us any further? I feel they will do no more, but people on the brink of ruin are capable of anything. (WND, 905)

People to Know

RYOKAN

There were many priests who vied for power and influence during Nichiren's time. The most prominent was Ryokan, whom the ruling family often asked to pray to bring rain or ward off invasion. Nichiren publicly declared that Ryokan, with his shallow beliefs and prayer, could never bring this about. When Ryokan's attempts failed and he was humiliated, he conspired to have Nichiren beheaded.

Even if it seems that, because I was born in the ruler's domain, I follow him in my actions, I will never follow him in my heart. (WND, 579)

The government's persecution of me has clearly demonstrated my faith in the Lotus Sutra. There is no doubt that the moon wanes and waxes, and that the tide ebbs and flows. In my case, too, since punishment has already occurred, benefit must be forthcoming. What is there to lament? (WND, 194)

The reason you have not succeeded in attaining Buddhahood from countless distant kalpas in the past down to the present is that when a situation such as this has arisen you have been too fearful to speak out. And in the future as well, this principle will prevail. Now I, Nichiren, understand these things because of what I myself have undergone. But even if there are those among my disciples who understand them, they fear the accusations of the times; believing that their lives, which are as frail as dew, are in fact to be relied upon, they backslide, keep their beliefs hidden in their hearts, or behave in other such ways. (WND, 1021)

Strengthen your faith now more than ever. Anyone who teaches the principles of Buddhism to others is bound to incur hatred from men and women, priests and nuns. Let them say what they will. Entrust yourself to the golden teachings of the Lotus Sutra, Shakyamuni Buddha, T'ien-t'ai, Miao-lo, Dengyo, and Chang-an. This is what is signified by the expression, "practicing according to the Buddha's teachings." (WND, 626)

Only one who has met with great persecution can be said to have mastered the Lotus Sutra. (WND, 799)

In a future age after the passing of the Buddha, there are bound to be persecutions and difficulties even greater and more fearful than those that occurred during his lifetime. If even the Buddha had difficulty bearing up under such persecutions, how can ordinary people be expected to bear them, particularly when these troubles are destined to be even greater than those that occurred during the Buddha's lifetime? (WND, 696)

By undergoing repeated persecution, just as is noted in the sutra when it says, "again and again we will be banished," I can erase the grave offenses of my past and for the first time attain Buddhahood. I therefore engage in these difficult practices of my own accord. (WND, 194)

Were it not for the rulers and ministers who now persecute me, I would be unable to expiate my past sins of slandering the correct teaching. (WND, 305)

At that time the ruler of the nation, allying himself with those priests who slander the Law, would come to hate me and try to have me beheaded or order me into exile. And if this sort of thing were to occur again and again, then the grave offenses that I have accumulated

People to Know

THREE ATSUHARA MARTYRS

Three farmers were arrested, tortured, and then beheaded based on false allegations of theft during Nichiren's time. This incident marked the first time followers were persecuted by the authorities—rather than the Daishonin himself—in such a severe way. Their martyrdom motivated Nichiren to inscribe the Dai-Gohonzon for the enlightenment of all people.

over countless kalpas would be wiped out within the space of a single lifetime. Such, then, was the great plan that I conceived, and it is now proceeding without the slightest deviation. So, when I find myself thus sentenced to exile, I can only feel that my wishes are being fulfilled. (WND, 436)

The practice of Buddhism is always accompanied by persecutions and difficulties corresponding in severity to whichever sutra one may uphold. To practice the Lotus Sutra will provoke particularly harsh persecutions. To practice as it teaches, and in accordance with the time and the people's capacity, will incite truly agonizing ordeals. (WND, 770)

When an evil ruler in consort with priests of erroneous teachings tries to destroy the correct teaching and do away with a man of wisdom, those with the heart of a lion king are sure to attain Buddhahood. Like Nichiren, for example. I say this not out of arrogance, but because I am deeply committed to the correct teaching. (WND, 302)

Corrupt authorities of the day, jealous of the devotion to Nichiren, conspired and arrested twenty innocent rice farmers. Tragically, three were beheaded for refusing to renounce their faith.

The phrase "when his offenses had been wiped out" indicates that, because Bodhisattva Never Disparaging met persecution, he was able to eradicate his offenses from previous lifetimes. (WND, 199)

PERSEVERANCE

But during the repeated persecutions I suffered and throughout my two sentences of exile, you have demonstrated your resolve. Though that has been wondrous enough, I have no words sufficient to praise you for having written a pledge to carry through with your faith in the Lotus Sutra, in spite of your lord's threats and at the cost of your two fiefs. (WND, 823)

Urge on, but do not frighten, the ones from Atsuhara who are ignorant of Buddhism. Tell them to be prepared for the worst, and not to expect good times, but take the bad times for granted. (WND, 998)

Many hear about and accept this sutra, but when great obstacles arise, just as they were told would happen, few remember it and bear it firmly in mind. To accept is easy; to continue is difficult. But Buddhahood lies in continuing faith. (WND, 471)

Life flashes by in but a moment. No matter how many terrible enemies you may encounter, banish all fears and never think of backsliding. (WND, 395)

Carry through with your faith in the Lotus Sutra. You cannot strike fire from flint if you stop halfway. (WND, 319)

If a person cannot manage to cross a moat ten feet wide, how can he cross one that is a hundred or two hundred feet? (WND, 766)

PRACTICE

Though muddy water has no mind, it can catch the moon's reflection and so naturally becomes clear. When plants and trees receive the rainfall, they can hardly be aware of what they are doing, and yet do they not proceed to put forth blossoms? The five characters of Myoho-renge-kyo do not represent the sutra text, nor are they its meaning. They are nothing other than the intent of the entire sutra. So, even though the beginners in Buddhist practice may not understand their significance, by practicing these five characters, they will naturally conform to the sutra's intent. (WND, 788)

Reflections

FROM THEORY TO ACTION

"As far as the fundamental teachings of Buddhism and the Gosho are concerned, I hope that, regarding them as absolutely correct, you will first and foremost strive to put them into practice. I urge you to do so because this is the shortest route to understanding the essence of Buddhism from the depths of your life." —Daisaku Ikeda

One who, on hearing the teachings of the Lotus Sutra, makes even greater efforts in faith is a true seeker of the way. T'ien-t'ai states, "From the indigo, an even deeper blue." This passage means that, if one dyes something repeatedly in indigo, it becomes even bluer than the indigo leaves. The Lotus Sutra is like the indigo, and the strength of one's practice is like the deepening blue. (WND, 457)

Those who fall into the evil paths because of their mistaken practice of Buddhism outnumber the dust particles of the land, while those who attain the Buddha way by practicing the correct teaching are fewer than the specks of dirt that can be placed on a fingernail. (WND, 400)

It is the way of ordinary people that, even though they spur themselves on to arouse the aspiration for enlightenment and wish for happiness in the next life, they exert themselves no more than one or two out of all the hours of the day, and this only after reminding themselves to do so. As for myself, I read the Lotus Sutra without having to remember to, and practice it even when I do not read its words aloud. (WND, 43)

PRAYER

Concerning prayer, there are conspicuous prayer and conspicuous response, conspicuous prayer and inconspicuous response, inconspicuous prayer and inconspicuous response, and inconspicuous prayer and conspicuous response. But the only essential point is that, if you believe in this sutra, all your desires will be fulfilled in both the present and the future. (WND, 750)

Nevertheless, even though you chant and believe in Myoho-renge-kyo, if you think the Law is outside yourself, you are embracing not the Mystic Law but an inferior teaching. (WND, 3)

Though one might point at the earth and miss it, though one might bind up the sky, though the tides might cease to ebb and flow and the sun rise in the west, it could never come about that the prayers of the practitioner of the Lotus Sutra would go unanswered. (WND, 345)

So, if you earnestly pray that blessings be given to you without delay, how can your prayers fail to be answered? (WND, 346)

Now Nichiren's lifelong prayer and desire will be achieved in an instant. And this fits the Buddha's prediction regarding the fifth five hundred years, just as

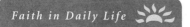

Faith in Daily Life

PRAYER IS DETERMINATION

Chanting Nam-myoho-renge-kyo is not beseeching an outside force for solutions but a means to muster our inner resources to meet life head on. It's an act of praising our own inner Buddhahood, or enlightened state, and causing it to come forth. Rather than begging or wishing, we chant with a strong determination or vow that we will solve our problems, make our dreams come true and fulfill our mission as Bodhisattvas of the Earth.

one half of a tally matches the other. (WND, 901)

Spare no effort in offering up prayers with firm faith. It is not that my resolve [to save you] is weak. Rather, it depends on the strength of each person's faith. (WND, 678)

We are told that parrots, simply by twittering the four noble truths of the Hinayana teachings, were able to be reborn in heaven, and that men, simply by respecting the three treasures, were able to escape being swallowed by a huge fish. How much more effective, then, is the daimoku of the Lotus Sutra, which is the very heart of all the eighty thousand sacred teachings of Buddhism and the eye of all the Buddhas! How can you doubt that by chanting it you can escape from the four evil paths? (WND, 141)

Therefore, we know that the prayers offered by a practitioner of the Lotus Sutra will be answered just as an echo answers a sound, as a shadow follows a form, as the reflection of the moon appears in clear water, as a mirror collects dewdrops, as a magnet attracts iron, as amber attracts particles of dust, or as a clear mirror reflects the color of an object. (WND, 340)

PROCRASTINATION

Deep in the Snow Mountains lives a bird called the cold-suffering bird that, tortured by the numbing cold, cries that it will build a nest in the morning. Yet when day breaks, it sleeps away the hours in the warm light of the morning sun without building its nest. So it continues to cry vainly throughout its life. The same is true of human beings. When they fall into hell and gasp in its flames, they long to be reborn as humans and vow to put everything else aside and serve the three treasures in order to gain enlightenment in their next life. But even on the rare occasions when they happen to be reborn in human form, the winds of fame and profit blow violently, and the lamp of Buddhist practice is easily extinguished. (WND, 1027)

Now I have already obtained birth in the human realm, something difficult to achieve, and have had the privilege of hearing the Buddhist teachings, which are seldom encountered. If I should pass my present life in idleness, then in what future life could I possibly free myself from the sufferings of birth and death and attain enlightenment? (WND, 125)

PROTECTION

I have carefully read your letter, in which you described the recent skirmish with powerful enemies. So they have finally attacked you. It is a matter of rejoicing that your usual prudence and courage, as well as your firm faith in the Lotus Sutra, enabled you to survive unharmed. (WND, 1000)

That is why the Great Teacher Miao-lo stated, "The stronger one's faith, the greater the protection of the gods." So long as one maintains firm faith, one is certain to receive the great protection of the gods. I say this for your sake. I know your faith has always been admirable, but now you must strengthen it more than ever. Only then will the ten demon daughters lend you even greater protection. You need not seek far for an example. Everyone in Japan, from the sovereign on down to the common people, without exception has tried to do me harm, but I have survived until this day. You should realize that this is because, although I am alone, I have firm faith. (WND, 614)

Had I not been exiled, but remained in Kamakura, I would certainly have been killed in the battle. In like manner, since remaining in your lord's service will likely be to your detriment, this may well be the design of Shakyamuni Buddha. (WND, 824)

Though the votary of the Lotus Sutra may be of humble background, the heavenly deities who protect him are fearsome indeed. (WND, 1133)

You must summon up the great power of faith more than ever. Do not blame the heavenly gods if you exhaust your good fortune and lose their protection. (WND, 1000)

Buddhism teaches that, when the Buddha nature manifests itself from within, it will receive protection from without. This is one of its fundamental principles. (WND, 848)

Reflections

EVEN A SINGLE SENTENCE

"Let's read the Gosho regularly. Even just a little is fine. Even a single sentence. Just opening the Gosho is a start. At any rate, let's strive to read the Daishonin's writings. It's important to have the spirit to study the Gosho, to open up the Gosho. Even if you forget what you've read, something profound will have been engraved in the depths of your life."   —Daisaku Ikeda

In the eighth volume of *Great Concentration and Insight* and in the eighth volume of *The Annotations on "Great Concentration and Insight"* it says, "The stronger one's faith, the greater the protection of the gods." This means that the protection of the gods depends on the strength of one's faith. The Lotus Sutra is a fine sword, but its might depends on the one who wields it. (WND, 953)

I recently received an official pardon, and I will return to Kamakura. Can this be the year in which the passage "What I long ago hoped for has now been fulfilled" comes true for me? Without your protection, could I possibly have sustained my life? Could I have survived to be pardoned? My life's achievements are due entirely to you and to those like you. (WND, 454)

Teach this doctrine to others clearly as I have taught you these many years. Those who call themselves my disciples and practice the Lotus Sutra should all practice as I do. If they do, Shakyamuni, Many Treasures, Shakyamuni's emanations throughout the ten directions, and the ten demon daughters will protect them. (WND, 978)

It is written that those who embrace the daimoku of the Lotus Sutra will be protected by the Mother of Demon Children and by the ten demon daughters. Such persons will enjoy the happiness of the wisdom king Craving-Filled and the good fortune of the heavenly king Vaishravana. Wherever your daughter may frolic or play, no harm will come to her; she will move about without fear like the lion king. Among the ten demon daughters, the protection of Kunti is the most profound. But your faith alone will determine all these things. (WND, 412)

QUALITIES OF
THE BUDDHA

Becoming a Buddha is nothing extraordinary. If you chant Nam-myoho-renge-kyo with your whole heart, you will naturally become endowed with the Buddha's thirty-two features and eighty characteristics. As the sutra says, "hoping to make all persons equal to me, without any distinction between us," you can readily become as noble a Buddha as Shakyamuni. (WND, 1030)

One feature of the Buddha is the unseen crown of his head. Shakyamuni Buddha's body was sixteen feet in height, but a Brahman of the Bamboo Staff school was unable to measure it. When he attempted to see the top of Shakyamuni's head, he was unable to do so. Bodhisattva Worthy of Upholding likewise was unable to see the top of the Buddha's head, and so was the heavenly king Brahma. Inquiring as to the reason, we will find that in the past the Buddha bowed his head to the ground in order to pay reverence to his parents, his teacher, and his sovereign, and he acquired this feature as a result. (WND, 332)

The foremost among the Buddha's thirty-two features is his pure and far-reaching voice. (WND, 332)

The Buddha has already been called a skilled physician, and the Law has been likened to good medicine and all living beings to people suffering from illness. The Buddha took the teachings that he had preached in the course of his lifetime, ground and sifted them, blended them together, and compounded an excellent medicine, the pill of the Mystic Law. Regardless of whether one understands it or not, so long as one takes the pill, can one fail to be cured of the illness of delusion? (WND, 132–33)

Showing profound compassion for those unable to comprehend the gem of the doctrine of three thousand realms in a single moment of life, the Buddha wrapped it within the five characters [of Myoho-renge-kyo], with which he then adorned the necks of the ignorant people of the latter age. (WND, 376)

RARITY OF ENCOUNTERING THE LOTUS SUTRA

You should realize that it is because of a profound karmic relationship from the past that you can teach others even a sentence or phrase of the Lotus Sutra. (WND, 33)

Truly it is more difficult to be born as a human being than it is to lower a thread from the heavens above and pass it through the eye of a needle at the bottom of the sea, and it is rarer for one to be able to hear the Law of the Buddha than it is for a one-eyed turtle to encounter a floating log [with a hole in it that fits him exactly]. (WND, 125)

From now on, all the beings in this world who are endowed with life will be able to embark on the ship of the wonderful and perfect truth and quickly reach the opposite shore. Zengi and the others of our group have met with great good fortune because of karmic bonds and have been privileged to hear these extraordinary words. Were it not for some profound karmic tie, how could we have been born in this sacred age?" (WND, 559)

Reflections ❻

FROM EXILE TO ACTUAL PROOF

"When the Daishonin was banished to Sado, quite a few of his disciples began to doubt, wondering whether his Buddhism was really true or not. However, it was precisely because he was exiled to Sado that he could prove in the way he responded to exile that he was the original Buddha and was able to complete so many important works."

—Daisaku Ikeda

Suppose one were to place a needle in the earth point up and throw down tiny mustard seeds at it from the palace of the great king Brahma in the heavens. One could sooner impale a mustard seed on the point of a needle in this way than encounter the daimoku of the Lotus Sutra. (WND, 143)

We do not know our past relationship with the mother who gave us birth, and we are unaware of when we ourselves will succumb to death. And yet we have obtained birth in the human world, something difficult to achieve, and have encountered the sacred teachings of the Thus Come One, which are rarely to be met. (WND, 100)

How fortunate it is, then, that even though we were born in the Latter Day of the Law we are able to hear the teachings preached at Eagle Peak, and even though we live in a remote corner of the world we are able to scoop up with our hands the water of the great river of Buddhism. (WND, 155)

How does the mirror of the Lotus Sutra portray the people who, in the evil world of the latter age, believe in the teachings of the Lotus Sutra just as they are set forth in the sutra? Shakyamuni Buddha has left us words from his golden mouth revealing that such people have already made offerings to a hundred thousand million Buddhas in their past existences. (WND, 1108)

We living beings, transmigrating through the six paths of the threefold world, have been born sometimes in the world of heavenly beings, other times in the world of human beings, and still other times in the worlds of hell, hungry spirits, and animals. Thus we have been born in immeasurable numbers of lands where we have undergone innumerable sufferings and occasionally enjoyed pleasures, but have never once been born in a land where the Lotus Sutra has spread. Or even if we happened to have been born in such a land, we did not chant Nam-myoho-renge-kyo. We never dreamed of chanting it, nor did we ever hear others chant it. (WND, 957)

A Buddha appears in the world once in countless kalpas. Yet even if one should meet a Buddha, it is far more difficult to encounter the Lotus Sutra. And even if one should encounter the Lotus Sutra, it is rarer still for an ordinary person of the latter age to meet the votary of the Lotus Sutra. (WND, 913)

The Buddha explained how difficult it is for a one-eyed turtle to find a floating sandalwood log with a suitable hollow, even after immeasurable, boundless kalpas. He employed this analogy to illustrate the rarity of encountering the Lotus Sutra. One should be aware, however, that, even if one should encounter the floating sandalwood log of the Lotus Sutra, it is rarer still to find the hollow of the Mystic Law of the daimoku, which is difficult to chant. (WND, 958)

REGRET

You must not spend your lives in vain and regret it for ten thousand years to come. (WND, 622)

Be diligent in developing your faith until the last moment of your life. Otherwise you will have regrets. (WND, 1027)

Awakening from my intoxicated state of slander, I felt like a drunken son who, on becoming sober, laments at having delighted in striking his parents. He regrets it bitterly, but to no avail. His offense is extremely difficult to erase. Even more so are the past slanders of the correct teaching that stain the depths of one's heart. (WND, 304)

Reflections

HUMANISM

"The Gosho is the jewel of humankind that crystallizes with diamond-like clarity the humanism of Nichiren Daishonin. Because this is an age of spiritual malaise, it is all the more important that we study the Gosho and return to the humanism of Nichiren Daishonin." —Daisaku Ikeda

Climbing a high mountain, I would shout these words aloud: "What has happened to Brahma and Shakra, the gods of the sun and moon, and the four heavenly kings? Are the Sun Goddess and Great Bodhisattva Hachiman no longer in this country? Do you intend to break the vow you made in the Buddha's presence and forsake the votary of the Lotus Sutra? Even if you fail to protect me, Nichiren, I will have no regrets, no matter what may happen to me." (WND, 660)

Any weakness in faith will be a cause for regret. The cart that overturns on the road ahead is a warning to the one behind. (WND, 497)

As you crave food when hungry, seek water when thirsty, long to see a lover, beg for medicine when ill, or as a beautiful woman desires powder and rouge, so should you put your faith in the Lotus Sutra. If you do not, you will regret it later. (WND, 965)

There have been instances in which those who governed a thousand or ten thousand *cho* of land had their lives summarily taken and their estates confiscated over trifling matters. If you give your life now for the sake of the Lotus Sutra, what is there to regret? (WND, 801)

SEEKING SPIRIT

For you to inquire about the Lotus Sutra and ask its meaning is a rare source of good fortune. In this age of the Latter Day of the Law, those who ask about the meaning of even one phrase or verse of the Lotus Sutra are far fewer than those who can hurl Mount Sumeru to another land like a stone, or those who can kick the major world system away like a ball. (WND, 922)

Life is limited; we must not begrudge it. What we should ultimately aspire to is the Buddha land. (WND, 214)

If you truly fear the sufferings of birth and death and yearn for nirvana, if you carry out your faith and thirst for the way, then the sufferings of change and impermanence will become no more than yesterday's dream, and the awakening of enlightenment will become today's reality. (WND, 130)

Since the remotest past up until now, you have merely suffered in vain the pains of countless existences. Why do you not, if only this once, try planting the wonderful seeds that lead to eternal and unchanging Buddhahood? Though at present you may taste only a tiny fraction of the everlasting joys that await you in

Fast Facts

FIVE MAJOR WRITINGS

Of all the writings of Nichiren, five are noted as particularly significant. They are:

On Establishing the Correct Teaching for the Peace of the Land—Draws a connection between the catastrophes of the day and erroneous views held by misguided priests.

The Opening of the Eyes—Explains that Nichiren is endowed with the three virtues of the Buddha in the Latter Day of the Law.

The Object of Devotion for Observing the Mind—Sets forth the theoretical basis for the Gohonzon as the object of devotion for attaining Buddhahood.

The Selection of the Time—Expounds that the Latter Day of the Law is a time when the teachings of the Lotus Sutra will spread far and wide.

On Repaying Debts of Gratitude—Shows how appreciation to one's teacher ultimately compels one to embrace and propagate the Three Great Secret Laws.

the future, surely you should not spend your time thoughtlessly coveting worldly fame and profit, which are as fleeting as a bolt of lightning or the morning dew. (WND, 64)

There is very little writing paper here in the province of Sado, and to write to you individually would take too long. Nevertheless, if even one person fails to hear from me, it will cause resentment. Therefore, I want people with seeking minds to meet and read this letter together for encouragement. (WND, 306)

You are indeed an unusual woman since you asked me to explain the effects of various degrees of slander. You are every bit as praiseworthy as the dragon king's daughter when she said, "I unfold the doctrines of the great vehicle to rescue living beings from suffering." The Lotus Sutra reads, "If one can ask about its meaning, that will be difficult indeed!" There are very few people who inquire about the meaning of the Lotus Sutra. (WND, 626)

SELF AND ENVIRONMENT

The ten directions are the "environment," and living beings are "life." To illustrate, environment is like the shadow, and life, the body. Without the body, no shadow can exist, and without life, no environment. In the same way, life is shaped by its environment. (WND, 644)

T'ien-t'ai says that one should understand that living beings and their environments, and the causes and effects at work within them, are all the Law of *renge* (the lotus). Here "living beings and their environments" means the phenomena of life and death. Thus, it is clear that, where life and death exist, cause and effect, or the Law of the lotus, is at work. (WND, 216)

You must quickly reform the tenets that you hold in your heart and embrace the one true vehicle, the single good doctrine [of the Lotus Sutra]. If you do so, then the threefold world will become the Buddha land, and how could a Buddha land ever decline? The regions in the ten directions will all become treasure realms, and how could a treasure realm ever suffer harm? If you live in a country that knows no decline or diminution, in a land that suffers no harm or disruption, then your body will find peace and security, and your mind will be calm and untroubled. (WND, 25)

If the minds of living beings are impure, their land is also impure, but if their minds are pure, so is their land. There are not two lands, pure or impure in themselves. The difference lies solely in the good or evil of our minds. It is the same with a Buddha and an ordinary being. While deluded, one is called an ordinary being, but when enlightened, one is called a Buddha. This is similar to a tarnished mirror that will shine like a jewel when polished. (WND, 4)

Neither the pure land nor hell exists outside oneself; both lie only within one's own heart. Awakened to this, one is called a Buddha; deluded about it, one is called an ordinary person. The Lotus Sutra reveals this truth, and one who embraces the Lotus Sutra will realize that hell is itself the Land of Tranquil Light. (WND, 456)

Because this mountain is where this wondrous votary of the Lotus Sutra dwells, how can it be any less sacred than the pure land of Eagle Peak? This is what [*The Words and Phrases of the Lotus Sutra* means when] it says, "Since the Law is wonderful, the person is worthy of respect; since the person is worthy of respect, the land is sacred."(WND, 1097)

SHARING BUDDHISM

One who recites even one word or phrase of the Lotus Sutra and who speaks about it to another person is the emissary of Shakyamuni Buddha, lord of the teachings. (WND, 331)

In the light of the Buddha's prophecy, "the last five-hundred-year period" has already begun. I say that without fail Buddhism will arise and flow forth from the east, from the land of Japan. (WND, 401)

Concerning the Lotus Sutra, however, the form of its teaching will vary depending upon the people's capacity, the time, the country, and the individuals who propagate it. Yet it seems that even bodhisattvas who have reached the stage of near-perfect enlightenment do not understand these relationships. How much less can ordinary people in the latter age ever fathom them! (WND, 1128)

The moon appears in the west and sheds its light eastward, but the sun rises in the east and casts its rays to the west. The same is true of Buddhism. It spread from west to east in the Former and Middle Days of the Law, but will travel from east to west in the Latter Day. (WND, 401)

One who attempts to propagate the teachings of Buddhism must understand the capacity and basic nature of the persons one is addressing. (WND, 48)

In the "Encouraging Devotion" chapter it says, "There will be many ignorant people who will curse and speak ill of us and will attack us with swords and staves." These passages imply that one should preach the Law even though one may be reviled and cursed and even beaten for it. Since the sutra so teaches, is the one who preaches to blame? (WND, 539)

I will teach you how to become a Buddha easily. Teaching another something is the same as oiling the wheels of a cart so that they turn even though it is heavy, or as floating a boat on water so that it moves ahead easily. The way to become a Buddha easily is nothing special. It is the same as giving water to a thirsty person in a time of drought, or as providing fire for a person freezing in the cold. Or again, it is the same as giving another something that is one of a kind, or as offering something as alms to another even at the risk of one's life. (WND, 1086)

Be that as it may, commit yourself to the Lotus Sutra and have faith in its teachings. You must not only believe in them yourself, but also encourage others to do the same, so that you may save those who were your parents in all your past existences. (WND, 964–65)

If Nichiren's compassion is truly great and encompassing, Nam-myoho-renge-kyo will spread for ten thousand years and more, for all eternity, for it has the beneficial power to open the blind eyes of every living being in the country of Japan, and it blocks off the road that leads to the hell of incessant suffering. (WND, 736)

In this entire country of Japan, I am the only one who has been chanting Nam-myoho-renge-kyo. I am like the single speck of dust that marks the beginning of Mount Sumeru or the single drop of dew that spells the start of the great ocean. Probably two people, three people, ten people, a hundred people will join in chanting it, until it spreads to one province, two provinces, and all the sixty-six provinces of Japan, and reaches even to the two islands of Iki and Tsushima. (WND, 672)

In view of all this, your sincerity in sending a gift of five strings of blue-duck coins whenever the opportunity arises truly entitles you to be known as one who propagates the daimoku of the Lotus Sutra in Japan. As first one person, then two persons, then a thousand, ten thousand, a hundred thousand, and then all the people throughout the country come to chant the daimoku, before you know it, their blessings will accrue to you. Those blessings will be like the drops of dew that gather to form the great ocean, or the specks of dust that pile up to become Mount Sumeru. (WND, 672)

Little streams come together to form the great ocean, and tiny particles of dust accumulate to form Mount Sumeru. When I, Nichiren, first took faith in the Lotus Sutra, I was like a single drop of water or a single particle of dust in all the country of Japan. But later, when two people, three people, ten people, and eventually a hundred, a thousand, ten thousand, and a million people come to recite the Lotus Sutra and transmit it to others, then they will form a Mount Sumeru of perfect enlightenment, an ocean of great nirvana. (WND, 579–80)

Faith in Daily Life

PRACTICE FOR SELF AND OTHERS

Buddhist practice exists not only so we can become happy but also so that we can lead others to do the same. Practice for self and others, then, is like two wheels on a cart. If we want to make progress, both wheels should roll together in harmony. When we give hope and encouragement to others, we ourselves also grow, so though we speak of practice for others, it is we ourselves who ultimately benefit.

The sutra states: "If one [of these good men or good women in the time after I have passed into extinction] is able to secretly expound the Lotus Sutra to one person, even one phrase of it, then you should know that he or she is the envoy of the Thus Come One. He has been dispatched by the Thus Come One and carries out the Thus Come One's work." Who else but us can this possibly refer to? (WND, 385)

I entrust you with the propagation of Buddhism in your province. (WND, 1117)

SINCERITY

The snow has fallen and piled up in great quantity. Even those with a strong resolve find it difficult to visit me. The fact that you have sent a messenger to me here shows that yours is certainly no ordinary sincerity! (WND, 1103–04)

Persons like you and her do not have full knowledge of the Buddhist teachings, and it pains me to think how greatly you must regret that you ever chose to follow Nichiren. And yet, contrary to what might be expected, I hear that you two are even firmer and more dedicated in your faith than I myself, which is indeed no ordinary matter. I wonder if Shakyamuni Buddha himself may have entered your hearts, and it moves me so that I can barely restrain my tears. (WND, 436)

We live today in a time of trouble, when there is little that ordinary people can do. And yet, busy as you are, in your sincerity you have sent me thick-stemmed bamboo shoots of the moso variety as offerings to the Lotus Sutra here in the mountains. Surely you are sowing good seeds in a field of fortune. My tears never cease to flow when I think of it. (WND, 1134)

The human mind is inconstant; it is ever-changing and unfixed. I thought it wondrous that you pledged faith in my teachings while I was in the province of Sado, and your sincerity in sending your husband all the way here is even more remarkable. The provinces we live in are far apart, and months and years have passed, so I was concerned that you might slacken in your resolve. However, you are increasingly demonstrating the depth of your faith and accumulating good deeds. Surely this is not a result of practice over just one or two previous lifetimes. (WND, 491)

SPEAKING OUT

You should always talk with each other to free yourselves from the sufferings of birth and death and attain the pure land of Eagle Peak, where you will nod to each other and speak in one mind. The sutra reads, "Before the multitude they seem possessed of the three poisons or manifest the signs of distorted views. My disciples in this manner use expedient means to save living beings." (WND, 909)

I knew from the outset that, if I set aside my fears and declared things exactly as they are, I would be sentenced to death. And even if I should escape the death penalty, I would surely be condemned to exile. So great is the debt of gratitude I owe the Buddha, however, that I have not let others intimidate me, but have spoken out. (WND, 529)

Moreover, Emperor T'ai-tsung was a worthy ruler, but he placed extraordinary faith in the teachings of

Nichiren's audience at his first lecture was surprised
at his declaration of the Lotus Sutra as the
correct Buddhist teaching.

Hsüan-tsang. As a result, though there were those who might have wished to speak out in protest, they were, as is too often the case, awed by the authority of the throne and held their peace. Thus, regrettable as it is to relate, the Lotus Sutra was thrust aside. (WND, 700)

However great the good causes one may make, or even if one reads and copies the entirety of the Lotus Sutra a thousand or ten thousand times, or attains the way of perceiving three thousand realms in a single moment of life, if one fails to denounce the enemies of the Lotus Sutra, it will be impossible to attain the way. (WND, 78)

Even though one may resort to harsh words, if such words help the person to whom they are addressed, then they are worthy to be regarded as truthful words and gentle words. Similarly, though one may use gentle words, if they harm the person to whom they are addressed, they are in fact deceptive words, harsh words. (WND, 178)

If the lion is sleeping and you do not wake him, he will not roar. If the current is swift but you do not pull against it with your oar, no waves will rise up. If you do not accuse the thief to his face, he will remain unruffled; if you do not add fuel to the fire, it will not blaze up. In the same way, though there may be those who slander the Law, if no one comes forward to expose their error, then the government will continue for the time being on its regular course, and the nation will remain undisturbed. (WND, 715–16)

To hope to attain Buddhahood without speaking out against slander is as futile as trying to find water in the midst of fire or fire in the midst of water. No matter how sincerely one believes in the Lotus Sutra, if

Reflections

SPEAKING OUT

"Words were the driving force behind the Daishonin's struggles. In light of the sutras, he naturally concludes that his only recourse is to speak out."   —Daisaku Ikeda

one is guilty of failing to rebuke slander of the Law, one will surely fall into hell, just a single crab leg will ruin a thousand pots of lacquer. (WND, 747)

If I remain silent, I may escape persecutions in this lifetime, but in my next life I will most certainly fall into the hell of incessant suffering. If I speak out, I am fully aware that I will have to contend with the three obstacles and four devils. But of these two courses, surely the latter is the one to choose. (WND, 239)

If in this present existence I am so fearful for my life that I fail to speak out, then in what future existence will I ever attain Buddhahood? Or in what future existence will I ever be able to bring salvation to my parents and my teacher? With thoughts such as these uppermost in my mind, I decided that I must begin to speak out. And, just as I had expected, I was ousted, I was vilified, I was attacked, and I suffered wounds. (WND, 727)

Likewise the people of Japan, by becoming enemies of the Lotus Sutra, have brought ruin on themselves and their country. And because I proclaim this, I am called arrogant by those of little understanding. But I do not speak out of arrogance. It is simply that if I did not speak out I would not be the votary of the Lotus Sutra. Moreover, when my words prove later to be true, people will be able to believe all the more readily. And because I write this down now, the people of the future will recognize my wisdom. (WND, 615)

The Buddha has constantly warned us, saying that, no matter how great an observer of the precepts one may be, no matter how lofty in wisdom and well versed in the Lotus Sutra and the other scriptures, if one sees an enemy of the Lotus Sutra but fails to rebuke and denounce him or report him to the ruler of the nation, instead keeping silent out of fear of others, then one will invariably fall into the great citadel of the hell of incessant suffering. (WND, 1021)

STAND-ALONE SPIRIT

Let others hate you if they will. What have you to complain of, if you are cherished by Shakyamuni Buddha, Many Treasures Buddha, and the Buddhas of the ten directions, as well as by Brahma, Shakra, and the gods of the sun and moon? As long as you are praised by the Lotus Sutra, what cause have you for discontent? (WND, 464)

Despite the great risks involved, Nichimyo
braved the journey to Sado Island with her
infant daughter to see Nichiren.

One should not be intimidated by the fact that so many hold such beliefs. Nor does the truth of a belief depend on whether it has been held for a long or short time. The point is simply whether or not it conforms with the text of the scriptures and with reason. (WND, 168–69)

The most important thing in practicing the Buddhist teachings is to follow and uphold the Buddha's golden words, not the opinions of others. (WND, 393)

If one hopes to learn and master Buddhism, then one cannot do so without devoting time to the task. And if one wants to have time to spend on the undertaking, one cannot continue to wait on one's parents, one's teachers, and one's sovereign. (WND, 690)

At first only Nichiren chanted Nam-myoho-renge-kyo, but then two, three, and a hundred followed, chanting and teaching others. Propagation will unfold this way in the future as well. Does this not signify "emerging from the earth"? (WND, 385)

One cannot be sure that one will live until tomorrow. However wretched a beggar you might become, never disgrace the Lotus Sutra. Since it will be the same in any event, do not betray grief. Just as you have written in your letter, you must act and speak without the least servility. If you try to curry favor, the situation will only worsen. Even if your fiefs should be confiscated or you yourself driven out, you must think that it is due to the workings of the ten

demon daughters, and wholeheartedly entrust yourself to them. (WND, 824)

STUDY

Exert yourself in the two ways of practice and study.
Without practice and study, there can be no
Buddhism. You must not only persevere yourself;
you must also teach others. Both practice and study arise from faith. Teach others to the best of your ability, even if it is only a single sentence or phrase. (WND, 386)

With regard to the transfer of teachings, it is divided into two categories: general and specific. If you confuse the general with the specific even in the slightest, you will never be able to attain Buddhahood and will wander in suffering through endless transmigrations of births and deaths. (WND, 747)

Fast Facts

SHARING THE WRITINGS

When was the first collection of Nichiren Daishonin's letters published? One year after Josei Toda was inaugurated second president, the Soka Gakkai completed the first published edition of the *Gosho Zenshu* (The Complete Works of Nichiren Daishonin) in April 1952. It was Toda's desire to make the Nichiren's writings available to all lay believers.

I hope you will read this letter over and over again
together with Toshiro's wife. The sun breaks through

the pitch-black dark. A woman's heart is compared to the pitch-black dark, and the Lotus Sutra is compared to the sun. (WND, 315)

From the beginning, I pursued my studies because I wanted to master Buddhism and attain Buddhahood, and also to save the people to whom I am indebted. (WND, 202)

But in matters of Buddhist doctrines one cannot jump to conclusions simply on the basis of the eminence of the person involved. The words of the sutras are what must come first. Do not make light of a teaching just because the person who preaches it is of humble station. (WND, 109)

THREE POWERFUL ENEMIES

The votaries born in the Latter Day of the Law who propagate the Lotus Sutra will encounter the three types of enemies, who will cause them to be exiled and even condemn them to death. Yet Shakyamuni Buddha will enfold in his robe those who nonetheless persevere in propagating. Heavenly gods will make them offerings, support them with their shoulders, and carry them on their backs. They possess great roots of goodness and deserve to be great leaders for all living beings. (WND, 385)

Devadatta was the foremost good friend to the Thus Come One Shakyamuni. In this age as well, it is not one's allies but one's powerful enemies who assist one's progress. (WND, 770)

Of the three powerful enemies predicted in the sutra, the first indicates, in addition to the sovereign, district and village stewards, lords of manors, and the ordinary populace. Believing the charges leveled by the second and third enemies, who are priests, these will curse or vilify the votary of the Lotus Sutra or attack him with swords and staves. (WND, 468)

[The Devil King] knows that those who hear even a single sentence or phrase of the Lotus Sutra will attain Buddhahood without fail and, exceedingly distressed by this, contrives various plots and restrains and persecutes believers in an attempt to make them abandon their faith. (WND, 42)

Arouse strong faith, and do not heed what they say. It is the way of the great devil to assume the form of a venerable monk or to take possession of one's father, mother, or brother in order to obstruct happiness in one's next life. Whatever they may say, however cleverly they may try to deceive you into discarding the Lotus Sutra, do not assent to it. (WND, 81)

When I examine these passages, I know that, if I do not call forth these three enemies of the Lotus Sutra, then I will not be the votary of the Lotus Sutra. Only by making them appear can I be the votary. And yet if I do so, I am almost certain to lose my life. (WND, 53)

What is more, once you become a disciple or lay supporter of the votary who practices the true Lotus Sutra in accord with the Buddha's teachings, you are bound to face the three types of enemies. Therefore, from the very day you listen to [and take faith in] this sutra, you should be fully prepared to face the great persecutions of the three types of enemies that are certain to be more horrible now after the Buddha's passing. Although my disciples had already heard this, when both great and small persecutions confronted us, some were so astounded and terrified that they even forsook their faith. Did I not warn you in advance? (WND, 391)

Understand then that the votary who practices the Lotus Sutra exactly as the Buddha teaches will without fail be attacked by the three powerful enemies. In the more than two thousand years that have passed since the Buddha's advent, Shakyamuni himself, T'ien-t'ai, and Dengyo were the only three who perfectly carried out the Buddha's teachings. Now in the Latter Day of the Law, Nichiren and his disciples and lay believers are just such practitioners. (WND, 395)

Suppose someone, no matter who, should unrelentingly proclaim that the Lotus Sutra alone can lead people to Buddhahood, and that all other sutras, far from enabling them to attain the way, only drive them into hell. Observe what happens should that person thus try to refute the teachers and the doctrines of all the other schools. The three powerful enemies will arise without fail. (WND, 394)

When an ordinary person of the latter age is ready to attain Buddhahood, having realized the essence of all the sacred teachings of the Buddha's lifetime and understood the heart of the important teaching set forth in *Great Concentration and Insight*, this devil is greatly surprised. He says to himself, "This is most vexing. If I allow this person to remain in my domain, he not only will free himself from the sufferings of birth and death, but will lead others to enlightenment as well. Moreover, he will take over my realm and change it into a pure land. What shall I do?" The devil king then summons all his underlings from the three-fold world of desire, form, and formlessness and tells them: "Each of you now go and harass that votary, according to your respective skills. If you should fail to make him abandon his Buddhist practice, then enter into the minds of his disciples, lay supporters, and the people of his land and thus try to persuade or threaten him. If these attempts are also unsuccessful, I myself will go down and possess the mind and body of his sovereign to persecute that votary. Together, how can we fail to prevent him from attaining Buddhahood?" (WND, 894–95)

TIME OF PROPAGATION

Even though Buddhism is before their very eyes, if people lack the proper capacity, it will not be revealed, and if the time is not right, it will not spread. This is a principle of nature. It is as if, for instance, the tides of the ocean were ebbing and flowing in accordance with the time, or the moon in the heavens were waning and waxing. (WND, 467)

Buddhism spreads according to the time and the people's capacity. Although I may not be worthy of this teaching, I expound it because the time is right. (WND, 861)

Yet even the worthy men described in the non-Buddhist scriptures know that one must await the right time. The cuckoo always waits until the fourth or fifth month to sing its song. Similarly, we read in the sutra that these great bodhisattvas must likewise wait until the Latter Day of the Law to appear. (WND, 439)

A person of wisdom is one who, understanding the time, spreads the teachings

of the Lotus Sutra accordingly; this is his most important task. If a person's throat is dry, what he needs is water; he has no use for bows and arrows, weapons and sticks. If a person is naked, he wants a suit of clothes but has no need for water. From one or two examples you can guess the principle that applies in general. (WND, 518)

A hundred years of practice in the Land of Perfect Bliss cannot compare to the benefit gained from one day's practice in the impure world. Two thousand years of propagating Buddhism during the Former and Middle Days of the Law are inferior to an hour of propagation in the Latter Day of the Law. This is in no way because of Nichiren's wisdom, but simply because the time makes it so. In spring the blossoms open, in autumn the fruit appears. Summer is hot, winter is cold. The season makes it so, does it not? (WND, 736)

This teaching was not propagated in the Former or Middle Day of the Law because the other sutras had not yet lost their power of benefit. Now, in the Latter Day of the Law, neither the Lotus Sutra nor the other sutras lead to enlightenment. Only Nam-myoho-renge-kyo can do so. This is not my own judgment. Shakyamuni, Many Treasures, the Buddhas of the ten directions, and the bodhisattvas who emerged from the earth as numerous as the dust particles of a thousand worlds have so determined it. (WND, 903)

TRUTH

You may pile up dung and call it sandalwood, but when you burn it, it will give off only the odor of dung. You may pile up a lot of great lies and call them the teachings of the Buddha, but they will never be anything but a gateway to the great citadel of the hell of incessant suffering. (WND, 714)

Question: How can we discern the error of distorted views? . . .
Answer: It can be neither discerned with our physical eyes nor perceived with our shallow wisdom. We should use the sutras as our eyes and give precedence to the wisdom of the Buddha. Surely, however, if this standard is made clear, people will become enraged

and be filled with resentment. Let them do as they will. What matters most is that we honor the Buddha's words. (WND, 155-56)

Though evils may be numerous, they cannot prevail over a single great truth, just as many raging fires are quenched by a single shower of rain. This principle also holds true with Nichiren and his followers. (WND, 618)

Those who believe in this sutra, therefore, must have minds that are as straight as a taut bowstring or a carpenter's inking line. One may call dung sandalwood, but it will not have the sandalwood's fragrance. A liar never becomes a truthful person simply because one calls him honest. All the sutras are the Buddha's golden teachings, his true words. When compared with the Lotus Sutra, however, they are false, flattering, abusive, or double-tongued. The Lotus Sutra alone is the truth of truths. Only honest people can keep faith in this sutra, a teaching free from all falsehood. (WND, 324)

Fast Facts

TREATISES, LETTERS AND NOTES

The writings of Nichiren fall into three catagories: first, formal treatises, or lengthy discussions on doctrinal texts, sutras and comparisons between the Lotus Sutra and other teachings, usually more theoretical; second, letters addressed to lay followers giving details of the Nichiren's thinking and activities; and third, short communication, in the form of brief advice or encouragement.

Realize that the time will come when the truth will be revealed that both the person and the Law are unaging and eternal. (WND, 392)

As a rule, people in the world value what is distant and despise what is near, but this is the conduct of the ignorant. Even the distant should be repudiated if it is wrong, while what is near should not be discarded if it accords with the truth. Even though people may revere [their predecessors' doctrines], if those doctrines are in error, how can we employ them today? (WND, 155-56)

U

UNITY

All disciples and lay supporters of Nichiren should chant Nam-myoho-renge-kyo with the spirit of many in body but one in mind, transcending all differences among themselves to become as inseparable as fish and the water in which they swim. This spiritual bond is the basis for the universal transmission of the ultimate Law of life and death. Herein lies the true goal of Nichiren's propagation. When you are so united, even the great desire for widespread propagation can be fulfilled. But if any of Nichiren's disciples disrupt the unity of many in body but one in mind, they would be like warriors who destroy their own castle from within. (WND, 217)

Even an individual at cross purposes with himself is certain to end in failure. Yet a hundred or even a thousand people can definitely attain their goal, if they are of one mind. (WND, 618)

If the spirit of many in body but one in mind prevails among the people, they will achieve all their goals, whereas if one in body but different in mind, they can achieve nothing remarkable. (WND, 618)

Though numerous, the Japanese will find it difficult to accomplish anything, because they are divided in

Faith in Daily Life

IMPORTANCE OF UNITY

The path to Buddhahood lies in working in harmony with people dedicated to bringing happiness to others through the Daishonin's teachings. Often referred to as "many in body, one in mind," this spiritual bond is a relationship in which, through mutual aid and support, people can reveal their own unique potential and give full play to their individuality. Nichiren often urged his followers to be vigilant against those trying to disrupt this unity for their own selfish gain.

spirit. In contrast, although Nichiren and his followers are few, because they are different in body, but united in mind, they will definitely accomplish their great mission of widely propagating the Lotus Sutra. (WND, 618)

UNSEEN EFFORTS

As I have often before, it is mentioned that, where there is unseen virtue, there will be visible reward. Your fellow samurai all slandered you to your lord, and he also has wondered if it was true, but because you have for some years now honestly maintained a strong desire for your lord's welfare in his next life, you received a blessing like this. This is just the beginning; be confident that the great reward also is sure to come. (WND, 907)

What is hidden turns into manifest virtue. (WND, 848)

VICTORY

Buddhism primarily concerns itself with victory or defeat, while secular authority is based on the principle of reward and punishment. For this reason, a Buddha is looked up to as the Hero of the World, while a king is called the one who rules at his will. (WND, 835)

VIOLENCE

Every being, from the highest sage on down to the smallest mosquito or gnat, holds life to be its most precious possession. To deprive a being of life is to commit the gravest kind of sin. (WND, 667)

The foremost treasure of sentient beings is none other than life itself. Those who take life are certain to fall into the three evil paths. (WND, 460)

VOW

I vowed to summon up a powerful and unconquerable desire for the salvation of all beings and never to falter in my efforts. (WND, 240)

My wish is that all my disciples make a great vow. (WND, 1003)

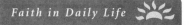

Faith in Daily Life

THE GREAT VOW

The vow of the Buddha is to lead all living beings to attain enlightenment, experiencing the most sublime happiness. Nichiren showed that through making such a great vow we can build a strong self. What's more, we can sustain our spirit, overcome our weaknesses and build a foundation upon which we can challenge all difficulties. Such a vow is an important foundation for our daily practice.

I will be the pillar of Japan. I will be the eyes of Japan. I will be the great ship of Japan. This is my vow, and I will never forsake it! (WND, 280–81)

Life lasts no longer than the time the exhaling of one breath awaits the drawing of another. At what time, what moment, should we ever allow ourselves to forget the compassionate vow of the Buddha, who declared, "At all times I think to myself: [How can I cause living beings to gain entry into the unsurpassed way and quickly acquire the body of a Buddha]?" (WND, 62)

WEAKNESSES

Even if the sun and moon should never again emerge from the east, even if the great earth itself should turn over, even if the tides of the great ocean should cease to ebb and flow, even if broken stones are made whole, and even if the waters of the streams and rivers cease to flow into the ocean, no woman who believes in the Lotus Sutra could ever be dragged down by worldly faults and fall into the evil paths. (WND, 70)

If a woman who believes in the Lotus Sutra should ever fall into the evil paths as a result of jealousy or ill temper or because of excessive greed, then the Thus Come One Shakyamuni, the Buddha Many Treasures, and the Buddhas of the ten directions would immediately be guilty of breaking the vow they have upheld over the span of countless kalpas never to tell a lie . . . . Thus a person who embraces the Lotus Sutra is absolutely assured of its blessings. (WND, 70)

It makes no difference if the practitioner himself is lacking in worth, defective in wisdom, impure in his person, and lacking in virtue derived from observing the precepts. So long as he chants Nam-myoho-renge-kyo, [the buddhist gods] will invariably protect him. One does not throw away gold because the bag that holds it is dirty. (WND, 345)

Human beings are equally vulnerable. They give their lives for shallow, worldly matters but rarely for the Buddha's precious teachings. Small wonder they do not attain Buddhahood. (WND, 301)

The human heart is like water that assumes the shape of whatever vessel it occupies, and the nature of beings is like the reflection of the moon undulating on the waves. Now you insist that you will be firm in this faith, but another day you are bound to waver. Though devils and demons may come to tempt you, you must not allow yourself to be distracted. (WND, 134)

WEALTH

In accordance with their status, some have wives and children, relatives, fiefs, and gold and silver, while others have no treasure. Whether one has wealth or not, no treasure exceeds the one called life. This is why those known as the sages and worthies of ancient times offered their lives to the Buddha and then became Buddhas. (WND, 1125)

Since nothing is more precious than life itself, one who dedicates one's life to Buddhist practice is certain to attain Buddhahood. If one is prepared to offer one's life, why should one begrudge any other treasure for the sake of Buddhism? On the other hand, if one is loath to part with one's wealth, how can one possibly offer one's life, which is far more valuable? (WND, 301)

How long does a lifetime last? If one stops to consider, it is like a single night's lodging at a wayside inn. Should one forget that fact and seek some measure of worldly fame and profit? Though you may gain them, they will be mere prosperity in a dream, a delight scarcely to be prized. You would do better simply to leave such matters to the karma formed in your previous existences. (WND, 63)

If you seek enlightenment outside yourself, then your performing even ten thousand practices and ten thousand good deeds will be in vain. It is like the case of a poor man who spends night and day counting his neighbor's wealth but gains not even half a coin. (WND, 3)

WISDOM

If one intends to repay these great debts of gratitude, one can hope to do so only if one learns and masters Buddhism, becoming a person of wisdom. If one does not, one will be like a man who attempts to lead a company of the blind over bridges and across rivers when he himself has sightless eyes. Can a ship steered by someone who cannot even tell the direction of the wind ever carry the traveling merchants to the mountains where treasure lies? (WND, 690)

[As a youth,] he received great wisdom from the living Bodhisattva Space Treasury. He prayed to the bodhisattva to become the wisest person in Japan. The bodhisattva must have taken pity on him, for he presented him with a great jewel as brilliant as the morning star, which Nichiren tucked away in his right sleeve. Thereafter, on perusing the entire body of sutras, he was able to discern in essence the relative worth of the eight schools as well as of all the scriptures. (WND, 650)

Bodhisattva Superior Practices received the water of the wisdom of the Mystic Law from the Thus Come One Shakyamuni and causes it to flow into the wasteland of the people's lives in the evil world of the latter age. This is the function of wisdom. Shakyamuni Buddha transferred this teaching to Bodhisattva Superior Practices, and now Nichiren propagates it in Japan. (WND, 746–47)

[The Buddha] teaches us to substitute faith for wisdom, making this single word "faith" the foundation. (WND, 785)

Is it not the meaning of the sutra and the commentary that the way to Buddhahood lies within the two elements of reality and wisdom? Reality means the true nature of all phenomena, and wisdom means the illuminating and manifesting of this true nature. Thus when the riverbed of reality is infinitely broad and deep, the water of wisdom will flow ceaselessly. When this reality and wisdom are fused, one attains Buddhahood in one's present form. (WND, 746)

WOMEN

While the Buddha was in the world, many women in their prime became nuns and devoted themselves to the Buddha's teachings, but they were never shunned on account of their menstrual period. Judging from this, I would say that menstruation does not represent any kind of impurity coming from an external source. It is simply a characteristic of the female sex, a phenomenon related to the perpetuation of the seed of birth and death. (WND, 71–72)

Only in the Lotus Sutra do we read that a woman who embraces this sutra not only excels all other women, but also surpasses all men. (WND, 464)

The dragon king's daughter represents "one example that stands for all the rest." When the dragon king's daughter attained Buddhahood, it opened up the way to attaining Buddhahood for all women of later ages. (WND, 269)

Fast Facts

DRAGON KING'S DAUGHTER

Nichiren often refers to the story of the dragon king's daughter. This story is found in the "Devadatta" chapter of the Lotus Sutra and speaks about the enlightenment of an eight-year-old dragon girl. This was a great feat since the common belief at the time was that women could not attain enlightenment. Thus, the Lotus Sutra, through the example of the dragon king's daughter, confirmed that all people could attain enlightenment without changing their basic character.

When the Thus Come One Shakyamuni expounded the Lotus Sutra in the saha world, this bodhisattva came to attend the ceremony and pledged to protect those women who would embrace the Lotus Sutra in the latter age. (WND, 911–12)

A woman known as the dragon king's daughter achieved Buddhahood through faith in the Lotus Sutra; she therefore pledged to protect women who embrace this sutra in the latter age. Could it be that you are related to her? How admirable! (WND, 960)

The sutra states, "If there are those who hear the Law, then not a one will fail to attain Buddhahood." This means that, even if one were to point at the earth and miss it, even if the sun and moon should fall to the ground, even if an age should come when the tides cease to ebb and flow, or even if flowers should not turn to fruit in summer, it could never happen that a woman who chants Nam-myoho-renge-kyo would fail to be reunited with her beloved child. Continue in your devotion to faith, and bring this about quickly! (WND, 1092)

Should these four great bodhisattvas desert the woman who chants Nam-myoho-renge-kyo, they would incur the wrath of Shakyamuni, Many Treasures, and the emanation Buddhas of the ten directions. You may be certain that their offense would be greater than even that of Devadatta, their falsehood more terrible than Kokalika's. How reassuring, how encouraging! (WND, 415)

Even if one were to meet a person who could cross the ocean carrying Mount Sumeru on his head, one could never find a woman like you. Even though one might find a person who could steam sand and make boiled rice of it, one could never meet a woman like you. You should know that Shakyamuni Buddha . . . and other deities will protect you, just as a shadow accompanies the body. You are the foremost votary of the Lotus Sutra among the women of Japan. (WND, 325)

A woman who embraces the lion king of the Lotus Sutra never fears any of the beasts of hell or of realms of hungry spirits and animals. All the offenses committed by a woman in her lifetime are like dry grass, and the single character *myo* of the Lotus Sutra is like a small spark. When a small spark is set to a large expanse of grass, not only the grass but also the big trees and large stones will all be consumed. Such is the power of the fire of wisdom in the single character *myo*. (WND, 949)

Reflections

TRUE LEADERSHIP

"Some of [the Daishonin's female followers] had lost their husbands. Some had lost their children, and others were caring for seriously ill infants. Some were facing obstacles regarding their husbands' work. The Daishonin sent warm, detailed encouragement to these women—all of whom were doing the best they could amid various hardships and sufferings. He strongly supported them. This is the mark of a true leader." —Daisaku Ikeda

But now you, born a woman in the evil world of the latter age, while being reviled, struck, and persecuted by the barbaric inhabitants of this island country who are unaware of these things, have endured and are propagating the Lotus Sutra. The Buddha at Eagle Peak surely perceives that you surpass the nun [Mahaprajapati] as greatly as clouds do mud. The name of that nun, the Buddha Gladly Seen by All Living Beings, is no unrelated matter; it is now the name of the lay nun Myoho. (WND, 1106)

Do not these interpretations make clear that, among all the teachings of the Buddha's lifetime, the Lotus Sutra is first, and that, among the teachings of the Lotus Sutra, that of women attaining Buddhahood is first? For this reason, though the women of Japan may be condemned in all sutras other than the Lotus as incapable of attaining Buddhahood, as long as the Lotus guarantees their enlightenment, what reason have they to be downcast? (WND, 930)

A woman who makes offerings to such a Gohonzon invites happiness in this life, and in the next, the Gohonzon will be with her and protect her always. Like a lantern in the dark, like a strong guide and porter on a treacherous mountain path, the Gohonzon will guard and protect you, Nichinyo, wherever you go. (WND, 832)

A woman who takes this efficacious medicine will be surrounded and protected by these four great bodhisattvas at all times. When she rises to her feet, so too will the bodhisattvas, and when she walks along the road, they will also do the same. She and they will be as inseparable as a body and its shadow, as fish and water, as a voice and its echo, or as the moon and its light. (WND, 415)

So if a woman makes offerings to the Lotus Sutra now in the last five-hundred-year period, [Bodhisattva Gladly Seen's] benefits will all be bequeathed to her without exception, just as a wealthy man transfers his entire fortune to his only son. (WND, 911)

Yet there is one river called the Sahaya that follows a course as straight as a taut rope, flowing directly into the western sea. A woman who has faith in the Lotus Sutra will be like this river, proceeding directly to the Pure Land in the west. Such is the virtue inherent in the single character *myo*. (WND, 149)

The Buddha promised in the Lotus Sutra that, for women, the sutra will serve as a lantern in the darkness, as a ship when they cross the sea, and as a protector when they travel through dangerous places. (WND, 614)

WORK

The Lotus Sutra states, "[The doctrines that they preach . . .] will never be contrary to the true reality." T'ien-t'ai commented on this, saying that "no worldly affairs of life or work are ever contrary to the true reality." A person of wisdom is not one who practices

Regent of the Kamakura shogunate, Hojo Tokiyori, was
concerned about myriad troubles facing the country.
Nichiren wrote to him about the power of the
Lotus Sutra to bring peace to the land.

Buddhism apart from worldly affairs but, rather, one who thoroughly understands the principles by which the world is governed. (WND, 1121)

Regard your service to your lord as the practice of the Lotus Sutra. This is what is meant by "No worldly affairs of life or work are ever contrary to the true reality." I hope you will deeply consider the meaning of this passage. (WND, 905)

For you, a lay person pressed for time in your lord's service, to believe in the Lotus Sutra is itself very rare. Moreover, surmounting mountains and rivers and crossing the great blue sea, you came to visit me from afar. How could your resolve be inferior to that of the man who broke open his bones at the City of Fragrances, or of the boy who threw away his body on the Snow Mountains? (WND, 1069)

To illustrate, it is like the case of someone in the service of the imperial court. Even though he may have served for a decade or two, if he knows someone to be an enemy of the emperor but neither reports him to the throne nor shows personal animosity toward him, all the merit of his past services will be thereby negated, and he will instead be charged with an offense. (WND, 78)

You had been forsaken by your fellow samurai and by the people close to you, and they mocked you for their own amusement. Under the circumstances, an official letter granting you any sort of fief, even one inferior to Tono'oka, would have been welcome. Yet, as it turned out, your new domains are three times as large. No matter how poor these estates might be, avoid complaining of it, either to others or to your lord. If you say, "They are excellent, excellent lands," your lord may add to your fiefs again. But if you say things like, "The lands are poor," or "There are no profits," you could very well be forsaken by both heaven and other people. You should bear this in mind. (WND, 945)

WORLDVIEW

Because Buddhism has gradually been turned upside down, the secular world also has been plunged into corruption and chaos. Buddhism is like the body, and society like the shadow. When the body bends, so does the shadow. How fortunate that all of my disciples who follow the Buddha's true intention will naturally flow into the ocean of comprehensive wisdom! (WND, 1039)

Thoughtful persons should examine the matter with great care. For if we put faith in writings that do not accord with the intention of the Buddha, how can we hope to attain Buddhahood? And if we follow such writings in offering prayers for the nation, how can we fail to bring about misfortune? (WND, 349)

When great trouble occurs in the world, minor troubles become insignificant. (WND, 306)

When we scrutinize the sutras and treatises with care, we find that there is a teaching about a precept known as following the customs of the region that corresponds to this. The meaning of this precept is that, so long as no seriously offensive act is involved, then even if one were to depart to some slight degree from the teachings of Buddhism, it would be better to avoid going against the manners and customs of the country. (WND, 72)

To speak out without fearing others and without flinching before society—this is what the sutra means when it says, "We care nothing for our bodies or lives but are anxious only for the unsurpassed way." It is not that one does not recall the calumny, the staves and stones that were suffered by Bodhisattva Never Disparaging. It is not that one is unafraid of the world. It is just that the censure of the Lotus Sutra is even more severe. (WND, 1017)

One should also have a correct understanding of the country. People's minds differ according to their land. For example, a mandarin orange tree south of the Yangtze River becomes a triple-leaved orange tree when it is transplanted to the north of the Huai River. Even plants and trees, which have no mind, change with their location. How much more, then, must beings with minds differ according to the place! (WND, 79)

Nichiren rose from a humble fishing village
community to reveal the way for all
people to attain enlightenment.

XYZ

YOUTH

If we consider the power of the Lotus Sutra, we will find perpetual youth and eternal life before our eyes. (WND, 413)

The bad luck of your thirty-third year will turn into the happiness of your thirty-third year. That is what is meant by the passage, "The seven disasters will instantly vanish, and the seven blessings will instantly appear." You will grow younger, and your good fortune will accumulate. (WND, 464)

Though still a youth, he followed in the footsteps of his sagacious father. And at an early age, having not yet turned twenty, he began chanting Nam-myoho-renge-kyo, and thus he became a Buddha. (WND, 1074)

Thus it was that the eight-year-old dragon girl was able to come out of the vast sea and in an instant give proof of the power of this sutra. (WND, 60)

Fast Facts

NICHIREN'S EARLY DAYS

Nichiren was born in a fishing village and started studying Buddhism at age twelve. His parents sent him to a Buddhist temple to study, and at sixteen he vowed to become the wisest man in Japan.

APPENDIX A:
LIST OF SIDEBARS

FAITH IN DAILY LIFE

(in order of appearance)

FAST FACTS

(in order of appearance)

PEOPLE TO KNOW

(in order of appearance)

REFLECTIONS

(in order of appearance)

APPENDEX B:

LIST OF
WRITINGS CITED

INDEX